THOSE WHO MADE A
DIFFERENCE

4

Terry Bosgra

Copyright © 2023 by Terry Bosgra

Cover design: Lana Bo

ISBN: 978-1-77883-074-7 (Paperback)

All rights reserved. No part of this publication may be reproduced, distributed, or transmitted in any form or by any means, including photocopying, recording, or other electronic or mechanical methods, without the prior written permission of the publisher, except in the case brief quotations embodied in critical reviews and other noncommercial uses permitted by copyright law.

The views expressed in this book are solely those of the author and do not necessarily reflect the views of the publisher, and the publisher hereby disclaims any responsibility for them.

BookSide Press
877-741-8091
www.booksidepress.com
orders@booksidepress.com

INTRODUCTION

Some people live a life that touches few; others live so that someone will be forever different whether unintentional or deliberate.

Sometimes by being an example, others go deliberately out of their way to improve and inspire all they contact.

My school teacher touched my life in a way that made me a different person, although I was young it affected me a lifetime.

It may be a parent, teacher, neighbor, or just a friend, that reached out to make your life better;

Some are gifted to change entire communities or nations. And in these pages, we only feature those who improved life.

This book is not intended to honor people like Hitler, Mao, Poll – Pot, Stalin, or Fidel Castro and others.

There may be disagreement about some; I know that having publicly commented on Mikhail Gorbachev in this line up, who was head of the "evil empire", but we must look at the big picture, willing to see past our own bias, and learn the whole story, we hope this book will do that. There are likely enough names to fill two more books.

All information in these pages have been compiled from public media such as Newspaper, Magazines as well as personal visits of about 30 or so individuals in personal interviews, and/or visits in our home, or their home or national meetings. The Purpose of this book is to inspire every reader to make a difference.

Terry Bosgra

About the Author

Terry Bosgra was born in The Kingdom of the Netherlands in 1935 and grew up in a family of 7 siblings during the cold winters when Germany occupied most of Europe and every family had to live on ration cards. For our parents it was not an easy time, but children are resilient and we came through it with few scars. There were no toy stores, meaning we became innovative and made our own from scraps we found in the fields rummaging through the trash heaps of the soldiers, we always found treasures there; for us it was more fun to make and invent our own toys.

The soldiers were everywhere, but many families lived in the country and were willing to take in an extra Jewish child. Communication and news-media was outlawed during WW-II, therefore information about the concentration camps, was not known, and only heard rumors or listened to a secret radio in the basement. In 1945 General Eisenhower opened all the camps to the media, saying: "*I want film crews, reporters, and all media to go in first, and document these atrocities so that none of this can be denied later.* "

In Amsterdam the Jewish parents were concerned with the seriously increasing dangers; Soldiers and traitors were always on the lookout for Jewish adults & children who were destined for Hitler and his bloodthirsty minions, eager to fill the trains that were headed for Auschwitz, Dachau, Buchenwald, and any of the 1000+ concentration Camps.

At the trial of Nuremberg it was clear that there were many guilty besides the key Gestapo leaders; Evidence surfaced that Hitler told Himmler: "*it is not enough for Jews to simply die; they must die in agony.*" Few were willing to stand up to the evil forces of the Reich, all lived in fear of their own safety, the guilt can not rest on Hitler alone, all of Europe is guilty; no one man can murder 6 million+ Jews. Hitler and his cronies had unchecked and absolute power.

At that time, children, as well as the parents, lived with a fear, (not so much of the soldiers, many were evil but some were kind); the real fear for us was the traitors among us, eager to please the enemy; people in this book such as Corry ten Boom, Anne Frank, and many others became victims of such evil people.

After WW-II, I joined the Marine Corps during the Korea War but as the hostilities in Korea, and in the South Pacific were winding down, we were temporarily parked in the West Indies of the coast of Venezuela. Actually not a bad place to serve for 3 years, I was planning to discharge there and move to Nicaragua, but dad called: (mom suffered with MS), and said: If u want to see mom, before she die, u better head for home. I did as dad suggested and was happy to see mom before she passed on. I stayed and worked <u>driving small tours through Europe.</u> During that time tried to immigrate to the US, but could not get in, due to an oversubscribed quota. Not wanting to live in Europe any more I moved to New Zealand. There fulfilled my lifetime dream of becoming a pilot, went to flight-school and got a license; Found, and married Pamela there, who became my life partner. (now longer then 60 years), We moved to California, and later to Honolulu; tried working at Pan-Am but needed more flight hours so went to work in finance, built my own financial business with great success; after 45 years sold it, and retired at age 70; then went to work with my friend Hal in Geneva doing humanitarian relief work in the Middle East & Africa. Got active in politics and am still running a daily commentary by internet running in about 60 – 80 countries. Hal (my amazing Partner) recently died, and the virus has kept me home in Honolulu. In order not to get bored and with no expertise I began writing these books about people who had deeply impressed me as I crossed their paths, (many in person), on my international travels, others as I learned about them.

During the 1970 I wrote Abortion the Bible and the Church, with much guidance from the legal and medical profession. It sold out 4 or 5 times. Due to the notoriety of the topic, it might have continued to be a high volume seller, but I did not have time for the required updates, (donated all funds to problem pregnancy organizations). In those days there was no email, we only had snail mail or telephone and long distance calls were expensive. The topic alone will continue to be in demand for generations to come, as accurately predicted by Dr Francis Schaeffer when he visited our home.

This topic; "*Those who made a difference*". Every person in here has been an inspiration to me, and I hope they are to u. This book has really two volumes of "*Those who made a difference*"; each book contains a one page story of about 200 or less people that have gone the extra mile to make this world a better place. All information is gleaned from the public information pages; read wisely and please help and join me to make our world a better place; God bless.

Contents

INTRODUCTION iii
About the Author v
Asha de Vos: (449) 1
Tjerk Hiddes de Vries: (450) 3
Athanasius: (451) 5
Kayleigh Mc Enany: (452) 7
Kyle Rittenhouse: (453) 9
Monica Gill: (454) 11
Christopher Rufo: (455) 13
Orrin Hatch: (456) 15
William Wrigley Jr.: (457) 17
Norman Geisler: (458) 19
Kate Middleton: (459) 21
Shannon Bream: (460) 23
Claude Pepper: (461) 25
Soren Kierkegaard: (462) 27
Queen Elizabeth II: (463) 29
Giorgia Meloni: (464) 31
Margrethe II, Queen of Denmark: (465) 33
Mary, Crown Princess of Denmark: (466) 35
Brother Andrew: (467) 37
Tulsi Gabbard: (468) 39
Everett Dirksen: (469) 41
Gladys West: (470) 43
Constantine the Great: (471) 45
John Wesley: (472) 47
Marcus Aurelius: (473) 49

Johann Sebastian Bach: (474) 51
Wolfgang Amadeus Mozart: (475) 53
Joseph Haydn: (476) 55
Giuseppe Verdi: (477) 57
Ngozi Fulani: (478)...59
Frederic Chopin: (479)..61
Theodore Beza: (480) 63
Hans Egede: (481) 65
Briet Bjarnhedinsdottir: (482) 67
Vigdis Finnbogadottir: (483)...69
Melania Trump: (484) 71
John Winthrop: (485) 73
William Prescott: (486) 75
Adam Smith: (487) 77
Pat Boone: (488) 79
Charles Hodge: (489)..81
Irving Berlin: (490) 83
Jerome: (491) 85
James Renwick: (492)..87
D, James Kennedy: (493) 89
Walter Williams: (494) 91
James Guthrie: (495) 93
Emma Lazarus: (496) 95
Don Knotts: (497) 97
James O'Keefe: (498) 99
Oliver North: (499)...101
Israel Kamakawiwo'ole: (500) 103
Emma Veary: (501) 105
Kirsten Flagstad: (502) 107
Kristan Hawkins: (503) 109
Danny Kaleikini: (504) 111

Alina: (505) 113
Nana Voitenko: (506) 115
Al Harrington: (507) 117
Yeonmi Park: (508) 119
Sirimavo Bandaranaike: (509) 121
Vance Havner: (510) 123
Ron Menor: (511) 125
J. Gresham Machen: (512) 127
Charles Stanley: (513) 129
Eddie Aikau: (514) 131
Eva Peron: (515) 133
R. C. Sproul: (516) 135
Arthur Lindsley: (517) 137
Allan Bakke: (518) 139
Vishal Mangalwadi: (519) 141
Ludwig II of Bavaria: (520) 143
Ernest Cassutto: (521) 145
Ann Coulter: (522) 147
Maria Bartiromo: (523) 149
Klaas Runia: (524) 151
Gabby Pahinui: (525) 153
Michelle Wie: (526) 155
Chloe Cole: (527) 157
Frank Pavone: (528) 159
Gerard Van Groningen: (529) 161
Marko Kropyvnytskyi: (530) 163
Joseph Boskovic: (531) 165
Svetlana Boskovic: (532) 167
Kirsten Neuschafer: (533) 171
Roy Moore: (534) 173
Kenny Poure: (535) 175

Kellyanne Conway: (536) 177
Nellie Bly: (537) 179
Richard Bong: (538) 181
Antony Armstrong-Jones: (539) 183
Beth Holloway: (540) 185
Boris Johnson: (541) 187
Ava Kolker: (542) 189
Hayley Mills: (543) 191
Carissa Moore: (544) 193
Stephanie Gilmore: (545) 195
Charlie Wedemeyer: (546) 197
Isabella Abbott: (547) 199
Chad Kalepa Baybayan: (548) 201
Nainoa Thompson: (549) 203
Mau Piailug: (550) 205
C. J. Walker: (551) 207
Ed Parker: (552) 209
Emmeline Pankhurst: (553) 211
Ka'iulani: (554) 213
Abigail Kawananakoa: (555) 215
Paul Revere: (557) 219
Pearl Kupe: (558) 221
James Dobson: (559) 223
Margarita Louis-Dreyfus: (560) 225
Clara Schumann: (561) 227
Alphabetical Page Book 4 229

Asha de Vos

(449)

Asha de Vos was born in 1979 in Sri Lanka; when she was about six-years of age her parents gave her second hand National Geographic magazines; as she perused these pages it made a deep impression on her young inquisitive mind and was inspired to become a scientist, study and go places where few had ever gone before and began dreaming of doing things none had ever done before and become an adventure scientist. Her primary education was at Ladies College, Colombo followed by the Colombo International School; she moved to Scotland for undergraduate studies in environmental and marine biology at St Andrews; she went on to gain her masters in integrative bio-sciences at the University of Oxford and a PhD from the University of Western Australia. Quite an accomplishment as she is the first and only Sri Lankan to gain a PhD in marine mammal research. De Vos served as a senior program officer in the marine and coast unit of the International Union for Conservation of Nature. She founded the Sri Lankan Blue Whale Project in 2008 which forms the first long-term study on blue whales within the northern Indian Ocean and doing that made an amazing discovery. It was previously believed that blue whales migrate every year, but she discovered through her research <u>that is not so</u>. Instead an unrecognized unique population of blue whales stay in the waters near Sri Lanka year-round. Due to de Vos research, the International Whaling Commission has designated Sri Lanka blue whales as a species in urgent need of conservation research and has started collaborating with the Sri Lankan government on whale ship strikes. De Vos is an invited member of the IUCN Species Survival Commission's Cetacean Specialist Group. She was a post-doctoral scholar at the University of California Santa Cruz and a guest blogger for National Geographic. She is the founder and director of the non-profit Ocean swell, Sri Lanka's first marine conservation research and education organization. She does believe that the health & future of coastlines must depend on local people, and argues that "parachute science", (the practice of Western scientists collecting data in developing countries and then leaving without training or investing in the locals of the region), is unsustainable and cripples conservation efforts. She also feels strongly that women should define themselves by their capacity and not let their gender limit their potential. She is a TED Senior Fellow, a Duke University Global Fellow in Marine Conservation and has been selected as a Young Global Leader by the World Economic Forum. In 2020 de Vos was named Sea Hero of the year by Scuba Diving Magazine. Her accomplishments are far more than can be listed on these pages. This lady is a trailblazing explorer and should be remembered as such by all those who love the ocean. We need her.

Tjerk Hiddes de Vries

(450)

Tjerk Hiddes de Vries was the son of a poor farmer born August 6, 1622 in Sexbierum (just the name of the town and has nothing to do with sex). According to grandparents I was named after him, therefore you can see why my name was changed to Terry. Once I visited Sexbierum it's a local village of about 1500 people, where most occupants know each other. He went to sea at age 12 and in 1654 he had attained the rank of master. Apparently, he was fierce fighter and few ships survived when they faced him during the time the *Judith war*. In those days wars at sea were fought with fires not bullets. The goal was to capture your enemy's ship and if that failed, burn it, as a last resort although Hiddes was able to get on board and capture 3 enemy ships and was rewarded the highest rank such as extraordinary captain with the admiralty of Frisia one of five autonomous Dutch admiralties. During the second Anglo-Dutch War, he commanded 11 cities in the battle of Lowestoft. He was able to free his ship from an entanglement of three burning vessels. A lot of the sea battles in those days were with the Swedes and the Norwegians; there were few who could outmaneuver Hiddes on the water. For his heroic actions, he was honored as a hero by the populace. It was common in our family to credit him with a high number of victorious battles at the sea; therefore, it might have been a bit an honor to be named after him. Although it was customary to name the children after family members and so were we. My oldest sister was named after mother's mother and the next person my oldest brother was named after the father's father. Whether or not the names were popular, nice, liked, was not an issue; that seems to have changed with newer generations; although we had lived thousands of miles from our roots there were a few frowns when we did not follow the family practice; I think some understood that my wife was not raised in that culture and when our youngest son was born several hours early, we had to scramble to dream up a name for him. So here is what came out of that. My younger brother Jan had just died in a tragic auto accident in Europe, so we decided to name him Johann and for a middle name we named him after our Chinese doctor and very dear friend. His name was Tung Kwang and we named him TK. After he grew up, he had to climb over many obstacles. Some do not allow initials, I remember him calling me from California saying TK is not acceptable they insist on the whole name in full, what do I do? Up to now I have survived with Tjerk as my first name and always used Terry. Tjerk Hiddes faced his final battle had his arm & leg cut off and even in that condition tried to rally his fleet. He was taken ashore where he died from his wounds. The country named 4 ships in his honor and erected at least 2 statues in his memory and a book was written.

Athanasius

(451)

Athanasius was born in Egypt in the year 296; his enemies tagged him the "Black Dwarf," that might have been the description of his physical body, but certainly not his intellectual capacity; the word giant might have been a better fit in that respect. The short dark-skinned Egyptian bishop had plenty of enemies. He was ordained a deacon at age 23; and soon after that he was a bishop; while still in his twenties making him most likely one of the youngest bishops that ever served in that title. He was exiled five times by four Roman emperors, spending 17 of the 45 years he served as bishop of Alexandria in exile. He was a guardian of the truth, being certain what he believed was the right theological position, but was he right? In the end, his theological enemies were exiled from the church's teaching and it is Athanasius's writings that shaped the future church; often the problem was his stubborn insistence of Arianism, (the reigning "orthodoxy" of the day was in fact a heresy, although at the time it was widely accepted and presented as truth. (Arianism is a Christological doctrine attributed to Arius, a Christian presbyter from Alexandria, Egypt; the theology holds that Jesus Christ is the Son of God who was begotten by God the Father with the difference that the Son of God did not always exist, but was begotten within time by God the Father, therefore Jesus was not Co-eternal with God the Father. All mainstream branches of Christianity have always condemned Arianism as heresy, thereby making Athanasius the chief defender of Christian orthodoxy in the 4th century, in that respect he was a pioneer of the Christian faith and in many respects stood alone, he is most known for defending the Deity of Christ. Athanasius was the first to list all 27 books of the New Testament, making him unique as one of the early church fathers, during a time that Christ's identity had been attacked since the 1st century; one of the earliest attacks came in the form of Gnosticism, which is a belief that only the "_enlightened_" could receive special knowledge from God, which was a select view. He was already embroiled in these controversies when he was the chief deacon assistant to Bishop Alexander of Alexandria. To Athanasius, the issues were not a matter of splitting theological hairs but Salvation was at issue. In Alexander's encyclical letter, signed by Athanasius (and possibly written by him), he attacked the consequences of the Arian's heresy. Although Athanasius lived 20 centuries ago, it is with great honor to list him on these pages. He died May 2, 373 in Egypt where he was a popular hero at the time when such issues were in the mainstream.

Kayleigh Mc Enany

(452)

Kayleigh McEnany was born on April 18, 1988 in Tampa Florida; her parents are Michael & Leanne McEnany, who own a commercial roofing contractor company. She attended the Academy of the Holy Names, preparatory school in Tampa. After graduating she majored in international politics at Georgetown University's School of Foreign Service in Washington DC and studied abroad at St Edmund Hall, Oxford; while there she was taught politics by future British labor politician Nick Thomas-Symons. After graduating from Georgetown, she worked 3 years as a producer of the Mike Huckabee Show; Mc Enany attended the University of Miami School Of Law for one year before transferring to Harvard Law School after completing her first year at the University of Miami. There she was the recipient of the Bruce J. Winick of Excellence; (a scholarship awarded to students in the top 1% of their class); she graduated from Harvard in 2016. As a college student she interned for legislators such as Tom Gallagher, Adam Putnam, and George W. Bush, and wrote media briefings at the White House Office of Communications, doing that while she was in law school, Kayleigh appeared on CNN as a paid commentator; and supported Donald Trump, although called his comments about Mexican immigrants racist. According to Michael

Marcantonio a fellow summer associate at a law firm she began supporting Trump after accepting Marcantonio's advice, in an interview with the NY Times; when Trump seemed to be the nominee she was told that a smart young blond Harvard graduate would be wise to be an early backer. On August 5, 2017 she left CNN and began hosting a 90-second webcast; _Real News Update_ on Trump's personal Face book page. Mike Huckabee called her a meticulous researcher; since her college days McEnany has been closely associated with the Republican Party and has been critical of the Obama presidency and has questioned his birthplace. She criticized Trump for being insensitive about the beheading of Daniel Pearl; In August 2017 the Republican National Committee appointed her as its national spokesperson. In 2020 she became the 33rd White House Press Secretary and was Trump's advisor from 2019 to 2020 a position she held successful until Joe Biden's inauguration as 46th president. After the Trump administration McEnany has been employed by Fox News as an on-air commentator. In her personal life she is a high risk of developing breast cancer and underwent a double mastectomy in 2018 she has authored a few books and is unquestionably a very high IQ lady who can think on her feet and belongs on these pages.

Kyle Rittenhouse

(453)

Kyle Rittenhouse was born January 3, 2003, in Antioch Illinois US. On August 25, 2020, multiple riots in Kenosha reached a boiling point when young 17-year-old Kyle felt enough is enough; and took to the street carrying his legal AR-15 rifle and knew how to use it, hoping to end the violence. He was a skillful shooter not just randomly in to a crowd but targeted only Joseph Rosenbaum, a 36-year-old man who had chased Rittenhouse into a parking lot and grabbed the barrel of his rifle, Rittenhouse then shot & killed him, Anthony Huber, a 26-year-old hit Rittenhouse over the head with his skateboard, Kyle shot & killed him; then Gaige Grosskreutz a 26-year-old with a pistol was shot in the arm thereby successfully disarmed him of a dangerous weapon. With quick & decisive action Rittenhouse seemed to bring the riots to a close, at least over there. 17-year-old Rittenhouse was charged with 2 counts of homicide and one count of attempted homicide and several other counts. He seemed to be the only sensible person while the rest of the city was out of control with looting, burning & killing. Kyle as a young Christian boy quietly submitted himself to the law. Public sentiment was highly polarized; multiple rightwing and leftwing politicians had answers what should be done with a young man like that. We all had questions, and watching these riots from an easy chair 5000 miles away we had answers and knew what should be done; what did Kyle do? He waited patiently in jail for a jury trial, of his pears the fairest American way to get justice. The 1921 trial lasted 19 days while the jury looked at all the facts of the riots, the young boy's age, the fact that he carried a rifle in the streets killed 2 people who attacked him and many more. I watched all the TV footage of the riots and saw the jury trial from A to Z. At the end of 19 days the jury (and I Terry Bosgra), came to the same conclusion and that was: <u>*Not guilty on all counts*</u>! The judge then polled the jurors and discovered that the verdict was unanimous; little is known about his family, or his education, and watching him throughout the trial, paying attention to every detail keeping his composure, very different from the highly charged rioters we had seen during the uprising. Kyle may not have been perfect but after seeing how he conducts himself at that young age I wished he was my boy and say that from the perspective of having worked with youth much of my adult life, Kyle Rittenhouse seems a young man who has wisdom; the scriptures are clear that Wisdom comes from God; Kyle Rittenhouse has been called a terrorist by some and a patriot by others; during the trial he showed us discernment, maturity, and a great deal of God-given wisdom.

Monica Gill

(454)

This story about Monica Gill first appeared in Faith & Justice, a publication of Alliance Defending Freedom (ADF) in May 2022, of which Michael Farris is President & CEO; some time ago we had the blessing of entertaining Mike as our house guest for a week of R&R in our home. Why is Monica here? She is now a teacher at Rockville Middle School in Maryland the place where she was assaulted grabbed her hair and slammed hard against a locker and left her there sobbing; she was just a mess. In spite of that early on she wanted to be a teacher, although her teachers often were exasperated but they clearly loved and respected their students, and wanted the best for them. They knew what was going on in our lives & connected with us, took special interest moving us up to the next level. My interest was not only in becoming a teacher but in the kind of teacher I wanted to be. The Lord placed that in my heart. She teaches history and government classes at Loudoun County high school in Leesburg Virginia; and greets her students every morning with a reminder that she loves them. A message over her classroom door: <u>*You are loved!*</u> I see kids who suffer academically and do not want them to have low self-esteem. She teaches 2 classes and prepare students for college-level coursework; trouble is 1/3rd of the kids cannot read above fourth grade level. Schools have been making decisions that seem far more ideological than really concentrate on what is best for kids instead of pursuing a political agenda. Then came the pressures, where Monica was forced to accept the fact that Charlie of yesterday is now Cindy, a boy is now a girl & vice versa. Monica could never cross that line. There are so many issues with that policy and as a teacher and a Christian were just untenable. As teachers we are supposed to be loving, respecting, and protecting, <u>*not harming*</u>. Now we are compelled to say things that are not true; it is not my intention to hurt anyone, but there are certain truths that we must face. We condemn these policies that damage children and defile the holy image of God. I love all of my students and will never lie to them. I am a teacher but serve God first. I will not affirm that a biological boy can be a girl and vice versa, it is lying to a child, it is abuse of a child and sinning against God. She found a few other teachers of kindred spirit. And together with Tanner Cross had the same opinion who had already begun working with ADF along with Kim filed a lawsuit in the district. It is an issue where the government is not only blatantly wrong but it's downright dangerous. Monica Gill you are a hero and may God bless you, Tanner, and Kim richly and win for the sake of all the youth of America.

Christopher Rufo

(455)

Christopher Ferguson Rufo was born August 26, 1984 He was raised in Sacramento his father Dino is from Italy and his mother Nanette is of Scottish ancestry. Both parents are attorneys; Christopher is a conservative activist, best known for his position against critical race theory, which he claims has pervaded every aspect of the federal government, poses an existential threat to the United States, and is anti-American. Rufo has been actively involved in Republican efforts to restrict critical race theory instruction or seminars. The theory considers the idea that racism is systemic in the United States through laws, policies, regulations, and even court decisions. Rufo describes his strategy to oppose critical race theory using the term to put all the various cultural insanities under that brand category, even when u read something crazy in the newspaper it makes you immediately think critical race theory. Rufo is also known for his opposition to LGBTQ education in schools, often claiming that public school are sexual abusers of children. Educators and investigative journalists have argued that Rufo has made such claims as part of an effort to provoke distrust toward public schools in order to promote school choice. Rufo graduated from Georgetown University Walsh School of Foreign Service in 2006. He was a visiting fellow for domestic policy studies at The Heritage

Foundation and a Lincoln Fellow at the Discovery Institute, (a Christian think tank known for its opposition to the theory of evolution and advocacy for intelligent design to be taught in public schools). In 2017, Rufo was a plaintiff in a lawsuit to prevent Seattle from imposing 2.25% income tax on sums above $250,000 a year for individuals and over $500,000 for couples. In 2018, he briefly attempted a run for the Seattle City Council. Through interviews with Tucker Carlson on Fox News, Rufo reportedly influenced the Trump administration to issue an executive order to prohibit federal agencies from having diversity training that addressed topics such as systemic racism, white privilege and critical race theory the administration described such programs as divisive anti-American propaganda. The ban was revoked by President Joe Biden on his first day in office. Divisions continued at the state level with Republican legislators putting forward bans on critical race theory. He appeared multiple times on *Tucker Carlson Tonight* and *The Ingraham Angle*. According to New Yorker writer Benjamin Wallace-Wells, Rufo's story on racially divided bias training sessions in Seattle was a "phenomenon" that helped to generate more leaks from across the country about the contents of courses and diversity training programs. He is married to a Thai-American who was once a computer programmer at Amazon Web; they live in Gig Harbor Washington with their 2 sons.

Orrin Hatch

(456)

Orrin Hatch was born in 1934 in the state of Utah and was chosen to represent his state as a US Senator from Utah and is considered to be longest-serving GOP Senator serving in the United States Senate. I visited his office and left my business card telling the staff that I would be back & left my cell phone number. I was in Washington in connection with the March for life, which I knew was close to his heart. He called me and asked if I could stop in tomorrow afternoon at 2 pm & I would get an hour of his time. That was more courtesy than I had received from my Hawaii senator. But at 1:30 PM on that day, I received a call on the cell phone that the senator had to return unexpectedly to Utah due to a death of a close friend, but had instructed his staff to tell me that if I would contact him the next time I was in town he would take me to lunch, which I thought was a great honor from a man with a schedule as busy as that of Senator Hatch. He knew I came all the way from Hawaii and assured me that it was important to him that we meet about the <u>March for Life</u> which was dear to his heart. We were never able to connect but the fact that we talked by phone in person and communicated by letter not through staff but in person was important to me, because I knew he was a man with a full schedule; only twice we spoke briefly in person once was at the *March for Life* and when I introduced myself to him, he said he remembered our connection and said don't let that meeting go I want to spend an hour with you. When Covit came all our travels did not end but certainly slowed down substantially. (Often times I say; if we don't make it here let's find each other in heaven). But I am Christian and Orrin Hatch was Mormon and we differed on the life hereafter so we will have to leave that to the Lord. As US Senator he authored and co-authored several pieces of historic legislation such as the *Religious Freedom Restoration Act*, the *State Children's Health Insurance Program* and the *Americans with Disabilities Act*. Orrin Hatch was known for looking out for the people who often did not have a voice in our laws and our country. In the few times I have spoken with him I had the distinct feeling that he wanted to hear what I had to say. Orrin Hatch personified the American Dream; the son of a carpenter he overcame the poverty of his youth to become a United States Senator; with the hardships of his upbringing always fresh in his mind he made it his life's mission to expand freedom and opportunity for others, from tax & trade to religious liberty and healthcare ....few legislators have had greater impact on American life than Orrin Hatch has had, he was a true warrior for our country, for liberty, and for his beloved state of Utah; he was a man of wisdom, kindness, character, and compassion; he died on Saturday, April 24, 2022, at age 88 we miss him.

William Wrigley Jr.

(457)

William Mills Wrigley Jr. was born Sept. 30, 1861 in Philadelphia, Pennsylvania, US. The families were Quakers of English descent. In 1891, Wrigley moved to Chicago to go into business for himself, he had $32 to his name. ($931 in 2021 money). He formed a business to sell Wrigley's Scouring Soap; and with the soap he offered a small premium of baking powder, as an incentive to buy his soap. The baking powder was more popular than the soap and being sensitive to market demands he began to sell baking powder and giving each customer two packages of chewing gum with a can of baking powder. Again, he discovered that the premium was more popular than the base product; and his company responded to market demands and began to concentrate on the manufacture and sale of chewing gum. In that business Wrigley made his name & fortune. He then set his site on a small Island Santa Catalina of the coast of Long Beach California; he bought controlling interest in 1919 and developed the Island with public utilities, new steamships, a hotel, the casino building an extensive planting of trees and scrubs and flowers and created an enterprise that would help employ local residents, by making use of clay and minerals products found on the island at a beach near Avalon; in 1927 he created the Pebbly Beach Quarry and

Tile Plant. Along with creating jobs for Avalon residents, the plant also supplied material for Wrigley's numerous building projects on the island; after building the Avalon Casino in 1929 the Catalina clay products Tile & pottery plant began producing glazed tiles, dinnerware, and other household items such as bookends. He also established the Wrigley Botanical Gardens on the Island. In 1924 the film: *Vanishing American* or *the Thundering Herd* For the movie 15 head of Bison were imported to be filmed; the movie did not do well and the funds were not available to return them and over the years the herd grew in to the 1000's they were trimmed down; the island can comfortably support a herd of about 150 bison's. the difference between Bison and Buffalo in general the Buffalo is mostly native to Africa and is generally slightly larger than the Bison although the Bison can weigh up to 1800 lbs. and can run up to 35 mph. they are not pets and should be treated as a wild animal and can be defensive if they feel threatened. Its best to keep at least 100 ft away from any bison and a selfie is not worth your life. Wrigley left his imprint on America leaving behind the Wrigley bldg. in Chicago, the name is synonymous with Chicago he left behind a legacy of leadership. William Wrigley Jr died January 26, 1932 in Phoenix Arizona.

Norman Geisler

(458)

Norman Leo Geisler was born on July 21, 1932 in Warren Michigan US, a suburb of Detroit. He attended a nondenominational Evangelical church from age nine, but was not converted until the age of eighteen. After that he immediately began to share his faith with others in various evangelistic endeavors – door to door, street meetings, jail services, rescue missions, and whatever venues Youth for Christ offered. He soon began to realize that he needed to find better answers to the objections he was hearing. This prompted him to a lifetime of Biblical study, and went to Trinity Evangelical Divinity School and Trinity College. He subsequently earned two bachelor's degrees, two masters and a Doctorate degree. Geysler's decades pursuit of knowledge overlapped a professional career which begun at Detroit Bible College (1963-1966); His education included Th.B. (1964) from William Tyndale College; and continued at Trinity College (1970-1971) He was later Chairman of Philosophy of Religion at Trinity Evangelical Divinity School and Professor of Systematic Theology at Dallas Theological Seminary (1979 – 1988). In 1981, Geisler testified at "the Scopes II trial" McLean v. *Arkansas Board of Education*. Duane Gish, a creationist, remarked: "Geisler was the lead witness for the creationist side and one of its most brilliant witnesses.

His testimony effectively demolished the most important thrust of the ACLU. Unfortunately (one observer writes) no testimony, and no effort by any team of lawyers, no matter how brilliant could have won the case for the creationist side. Geisler was formerly a president of the Evangelical Theological Society (ETS) but left in 2003 when it did not expel <u>Clark Pinnock</u>, who advocated <u>*open theism*</u>. (Usually refers to Monotheism <u>*(one God)*</u> as opposed to <u>Pantheism</u> <u>*(many gods)*</u> and <u>Atheism</u> <u>*no God*</u>. In 1997, Geisler co-authored <u>When Cultists Ask;</u> <u>*a popular Handbook on Cultic Misinterpretation*</u> He contributed to: <u>The Counterfeit Gospel of Mormonism</u>. In 2008, Geisler co-founded the Veritas Evangelical Seminary located in Santa Ana, California. The seminary offers master's degrees in theological studies. Apologetics, Biblical Studies & Divinity. Geisler served as Chancellor, Distinguished Professor of Apologetics, and Theology and occupant of the Norman Geisler Chair of Christian Apologetics. He retired from his post in May 2019 and is mostly known as a Classical Christian Apologist. Between 1970 and 1990 he participated in dozens of public debates and gained a reputation as a defender of biblical miracles, the resurrection of Jesus, and the reliability of the Bible. He was married to Barbara Jean and together they had six children. Norman Geisler died of cerebral thrombosis at a hospital in Charlotte, North Carolina on July 1, 2019, 20 days before his 87th birthday.

Kate Middleton

(459)

Kate Middleton was born 9 January 1982 in Berkshire England, went to school and grew up there. The Middleton family had emigrated from Jordan in 1984 where her father worked for British Airways. He had married into the British aristocracy and benefited financially from a 100-year-old trust fund. Kate was enrolled in St Andrews private boarding school at age 4 and there she displayed talents in sports, and was captain of the women's field hockey team. She is the eldest of three children born to Michael Middleton and Carole Goldsmith, and was offered a class at the University of Edinburgh, but decided on the British Institute of Florence in Italy and traveled to Chile to participate in a <u>Raleigh International Program</u>, (Volunteer overseas program.) While waiting, she worked as deckhand at the Port of Southampton during the preceding summer. Later studied history of art, in Scotland, and received the Gold Duke of Edinburgh Award. Kate took classes in retail & marketing. In college she met William in 2001. They were engaged while on a safari in Kenya and married on 29 April, 2011 at Westminster Abby before an estimated global audience of about 300 million; William is the oldest son of (<u>former prince now King</u>) Charles, who is in succession to the British throne. His mother was Princess Diane who died when he was age 15.

Catherine holds patronage within 20+ charitable and military organizations, including Action for children, Sports Aid, and the National Portrait Gallery. She undertakes projects through the Royal Foundation, with her charity work focusing on Disadvantaged young children, Addiction, Art, and Mental illness. She encourages people to open up about such issues, and envisioned a mental health awareness campaign with William and Harry, and called it "*Heads Together*" launched in April 2016. The media called Catherine's impact on British and American fashion the "*Kate Middleton Effect.*" In 2011, 2012, and 2013, *Time magazine* selected her as one of the 100 Most Influential People in the World. On 9 September 2022 she became Princess of Wales when her husband William was named Prince of Wales by his father King Charles III. Since her college days she has been active in fundraising for community projects every year and met William at a charity Fashion show while at the University and began dating the following year. The couple has 3 children, George, Charlotte, and Louis all who are titled Prince and Princess. She & William visited the UNICEF Division for malnourished children in Copenhagen, Denmark. Kate has devoted her life focusing attention on children who need it most; someday she will be queen and may be the greatest goodwill ambassador Britain has ever had.

Shannon Bream

(460)

Shannon Noelle Bream De Puy, was born December 23, 1970, and began her studies at Liberty University in Lynchburg, Virginia. When she was 17 years old; during her college years, she won the pageant title Miss Virginia in 1990. She then participated in the Miss America 1991 pageant.

Much of her undergraduate tuition was covered by the scholarship award money which took care of much of her tuition for the education. After graduating from Liberty University in 1993 with a degree in Business Management, *Magna cum laude;* Bream returned to Tallahassee and attended law school at Florida State University. She interned with Florida Congressman Bill McCollum at the US House of Representatives; McCollum later became the Florida Attorney General. While Shannon studied at the Florida State law school, she won the Miss Florida USA pageant (1995) and placed fourth in the Miss USA 1995 pageant; again, her scholarship awards from Miss USA pageants paid for most of her law school education. After graduation with a JD degree with honors from Florida State University College of Law in 1996, Bream moved to Tampa, Florida and began her new career as a lawyer practicing while specializing in race discrimination and sexual harassment. She eventually made a career change from the legal profession to pursue a career in television news. In 2001 she moved to Charlotte North Carolina becoming the evening and late-night news reporter for the CBS affiliate WBTV. In 2004, after three years at WBTV, Bream joined Washington D.C.'s NBC affiliate WRC-TV, there she was a weekend anchor and covered general assignments. While at WRC-TV, in Washington, Bream met Brit Hume, who was the managing editor of the Fox News Channel's Washington bureau; He encouraged her to apply at Fox News. She did and became the anchor/host of *Fox News@Night*.

Bream is the author of a number of books: *Finding the Bright Side*; *The Art of Chasing What Matters*; *The Women of the Bible Speak*; *The wisdom of 16 Women and their Lessons for Today* reached the number one spot on the New York Times Best Seller list.

Shannon Bream is Christian and from what I can see about her it seems that she is not just a church attendee, but is a committed and practicing Christian. She is a talented lady in what she does; and is a trained classical pianist. Her husband Sheldon Bream has a company that connects event planners with speakers, and is a brain tumor survivor. I saw her first on Fox News Television and immediately knew she is a very sharp lady. It seems evident to me that she has kept her humility in spite of all the fame & fortune, and has become one of my favorite TV personalities.

Shannon Bream you are a special lady.

Claude Pepper

(461)

Claude Denson Pepper was born 8 September 1900 in Dudleyville Alabama US, the son of a farming family. After graduating from Camp Hill High School, he operated a hat cleaning and repair business, taught school in Dothan and worked in an Ensley steel mill before beginning studies at the University of Alabama. While in college he joined the Army at World War I, and served in the Student Army Training Corps (SATC). The war ended before he saw action, but was able to use his veteran benefit to attend Harvard Law School and received his LL.B. in 1924. He taught law at the university of Arkansas where one of his students was J. William Fulbright. After that he opened a law practice; he was a member of the Florida Democratic Party's executive committee; in 1928 he was elected to the Florida House of Representative, but in 1936 he ran unopposed in the US Senate, and was re-elected in 1944, and in 1950 lost his bid for a third term, and returned to his law practice. Then in 1962 he did what almost no one had ever done before, he took a step down to the lower house and ran for the US House of Representatives and got elected, meaning the Florida voters must have really liked him, and he began publishing in 1984 a paper and called it "*The Pepper Report*": and became known as the "*Grand old man of Florida politics*"

and was featured on the cover of Time magazine in 1938 and 1983. Republicans often joked that he and the Speaker Tip O'Neill were the 2 Democrats who really drove President Ronald Reagan crazy. How did I get to know this man? I was visiting Hawaii Representative Spark Matsunaga who had invited me to the House dining-room and wanted me to try his favorite bean soup. While trying the soup Matsunaga was called to the House floor and felt bad to leave me alone so he took me to the table of Representative Pepper whom I had wanted to meet. He had just finished a study about "Drugs in our School" That morning I had come from Senator Eastland who had finished a hearing on the dangers of Marihuana. At that time, I was writing about Marihuana problems among our youth. Pepper gave me his findings as reported in the 100-page report titled "Drugs in our Schools". I did enjoy the bean soup but it was a greater honor to spent 3 hours in the House Dining room with Representative Claude Pepper. In 1989 he was presented the Presidential Medal of Freedom by President George H. W. Bush. Four days later on May 30 1989 Claude Pepper died in his sleep. To honor his memory, Miami put up a statue of his image. It was an honor to spent 3 hours with him face to face in the US House Dining-room in Washington DC.

Soren Kierkegaard

(462)

Soren Kierkegaard was born 5 May, 1813 in Copenhagen Denmark to an affluent family; his father was a well-to-do merchant from Jutland. The young Kierkegaard was interested in the philosophy of Christian Wolff and liked the comedies of Ludwig Holberg and was also a fan of Plato. He suffered from tuberculosis which eventually killed him. From age 8 to 17 he attended the Civic Virtue Gymnasium where he studied Latin, history and other subjects. It is generally believed that it was there that he was engaged to Regina Olson but could not do things half-hearted and broke off the engagement because he wanted to immerse himself fully to his writing career, he did not think it would co-exist with married life, although he claimed to be deeply in love with her. Some have said his relationship to women was questionable. We have always known him to be a mystical poet and the love and affection between a young man and a woman has been a puzzle for as long as God has allowed us to dwell on this earth and differs mightily among cultures and this issue along with many others about Kierkegaard shall remain a mystery to us, and shall leave it there. He frequently got into disagreements with fellow students and was ambivalent toward his teachers. He went on to study theology at the University of Copenhagen but had little interest in historical works, or philosophy all of which dissatisfied him. He said: I do not merely want knowledge, but want to be clear about what I am to do and what I must know. He did not want to be a philosopher nor did he want to preach a Christianity that was an illusion. He grew up in a home of old-fashioned hospitality, although he never mentioned his mother in any of his works, she died from typhus at age 66, but he did often write about his father who died at age 82. He generally steered away from politics but was critical of the women's liberation movement, and had strong leanings toward conservatism. Many of the 20th-century philosophers, both theistic and atheistic theologians drew concepts from Kierkegaard, special when he wrote about the importance of the individual. He was raised as a Lutheran, and his writings have had considerable influence on the 20th-century literature. If u like to know why he is listed here, may be this will confuse you as much as we are. Here are what others said about him: *He was the sanest man of his generation*; *He was the greatest Dane of the century*; *He was a Schizophrenic*; *He was the greatest Christian ever*; *He destroyed the Christian Faith*; *He was one of the damned who never found faith*; *He possessed the truth*; *He was the knight of faith*. After wading through such writings we have attempted to bring you a glimpse of his life that ended when he was only 42 years old in Copenhagen.

Queen Elizabeth II

(463)

Elizabeth Alexandra was born Princess Elizabeth of York on 21 April, 1926 in Mayfair, London England, as the first child of the Duke & Duchess of York, (later King George VI and Queen Elizabeth). As a little girl she was cherished by Grandpa King George, whom she affectionately called "*Grandpa England*", when he was very ill, she made regular visits to him, which were credited by the press with raising his spirits and aiding in his recovery; she was a teary-eyed toddler when her parents departed on a tour of New Zealand & Australia. Her only sister Princess Margaret was born in 1930; both were privately educated at home and Elizabeth had a lifelong love for dogs & horses. Winston Churchill described her at age two, as a character with an air of authority and reflectiveness, astonishing in an infant. During the reign of her grandfather she was third in line for the throne and began public duties during WW-II; in Nov. 1939 she met Prince Philip of Greece and Denmark when she was 13; eight years later they were engaged at her age 21, and on 20 Nov. 1947 they got married, which lasted 73 years until he died in 2021. They had 4 children: Charles, Anne, Andrew, and Edward. When her father died in Feb. 1952, she was 25 years old when she was crowned Queen of England and seven Independent Commonwealth

Countries. She reigned 70 years till her death, and was served by 170 Prime Ministers across her realms, (perhaps the most notorious one may have been Winston Churchill). Her visits and meetings included most Commonwealth Nations as well as China, Russia, even the Republic of Ireland, and met with 5 popes. Some significant events were the Coronation in 1953, and the Silver, Golden, Diamond, and Platinum, Jubilees respectively. Her family was supportive, but there were several breakdowns beginning with the lives of her sister Margaret who's 20-year marriage to Photographer Armstrong-Jones was filled with multiple affairs carried out by both parties, and more noticeably was the failed marriage of her son Charles and his popular wife Diana, also plagued with numerous affairs on both sides followed by divorce and later a horrific auto accident which Diana was killed. Little was known about the Queen's personal feelings who rarely gave interviews and, never expressed opinions to the media. She was patron of more than 600 charities & organizations, and helped raise over 1.4 billion pounds during her reign. She took the coronation oath seriously, was deeply religious and committed to her civic duties as well as her regular worship at the Church of England of which she was Supreme Governor. Queen Elizabeth died at age 96 in Scotland on 8 Sept, 2022. Royal historians believe she had hoped that the rift between William and Harry would heal before she died. It did <u>not</u> happen; perhaps the Queen's family was more normal than we like to believe.

Giorgia Meloni
(464)

Giorgia Meloni was born 15 Jan. 1977 in Rome Italy; her mother is from Sicily and her father from Sardinia, but he left when she was 11 years old. In 1992 at age 15 she joined the Youth Front, (*the younger wing of the Italian Social Movement*) and there made a name for herself, and look so good, some thought she could be the future Prime Minister, which would make her the first woman ever to serve in that position. Her political positions all pointed in that direction. She is a Conservative Catholic Christian, and has positioned herself to defend God, the Fatherland, is Pro Family, is against Abortion & Euthanasia, and strongly opposes Same Sex Marriage, nor should such people adopt children, Italy needs strong nuclear families with Male Fathers and Female Mothers. She condemned the Russian invasion of Ukraine, and voted to send arms there. She has become a breath of fresh air on the European political scene, in the home country of the Catholic Church, even though the Pope lives there, Italy has drifted far left. While being active politically, she worked as a Nanny, Waitress, and Bartender, at the Piper Club, (one of the most famous nightclubs in Rome), she graduated from a technical high school specializing in the tourist industry. In the 2006 general election, she won a seat at the Chamber of Deputies as a member of the National Alliance, and became its youngest ever vice-president, in that same year began working as a journalist. In August 2008 she challenged the Italian athletes to boycott the opening ceremony of the Beijing Olympic Games in protest of China's policy toward Tibet; in that same year she voted in favor of a decree law against Euthanasia; and took over the presidency of the United Party's Youth Section, called Young Italy. In 2010 she presented a 300 million euro package called: the _Right to the Future_, it was aimed at investing in the lives of young entrepreneurs and coordinated with like-minded individuals who had similar ambitions. In 2012 she founded a new political movement: "Brothers of Italy, (FdI), and in the 2013 election got 9 seats and the next year was nominated as the Party leader, receiving 348,700 votes. In 2016 she participated in a major anti-LGBT rights demonstration declaring her strong opposition to that and won 20.6% of the vote almost twice that of the opposition. She won a debate against the Prime Minister Matteo Renzi and was favored with 60% of the vote. To strengthen the party she formed an alliance putting her in very strong position to lead Italy. We would love to import her to the US, but is needed to be a strong conservative voice in Europe now that Angela Merkel after 16 years has stepped back.

Margrethe II, Queen of Denmark

(465)

One week after Nazi Germany invaded Denmark on 9 April 1940, Princess Margrethe was born on 16 April 1940, in the royal residence of her parents at Amalienborg palace in central Copenhagen. Upon the death of her father who died on 14 January 1972, (*and after a required constitutional amendment allowing women to inherit the throne*), she became the first female monarch of Denmark. She is known for her strong archaeological passion and has participated in several excavations in Denmark, Italy, Egypt, and South America. As Queen she has received 42 official state visits, and has undertaken 55 foreign state visits herself and her support in Denmark as well as in most of Europe has consistently remained high at around 82%, as well as her personal popularity. Now that British Queen Elizabeth is gone, Margrethe who has reigned as Denmark's monarch for over 50 years, she is the world's only current queen regnant, while King Charles is re-structuring the British monarchy, all European Royal houses are taking a serious look at their own Royal family lines; many beginning to slim down the monarchies, especially when dealing with 2nd marriages among their offspring; all are watching with baited breath every move of the British King, who is sending shockwaves through that generation in most of Europe, including the Royals of Denmark, there is serious concern, all eyes are on every move of the British monarch anxiously awaiting what he will do next; their own security was never in question, but is now on shaky ground. All of them had private education by the sharpest minds in the kingdom. Queen Margrethe for example is well educated, well-traveled, and is fluent in many languages, such as Danish, French, English, Swedish, German, and has limited knowledge of Faroese, (*Island group between Iceland & Norway, part of Denmark but maintain their own language*). She was privately educated and spent a few years at boarding schools for girls in Hampshire England, as well as studied economics in London and took post-studies in prehistoric archaeology at Girton College in Cambridge. In London she met French diplomat, Henri-Andre de Monpezat and married him later at the Holmen church in Copenhagen, His title became: "His Royal Highness Prince Henrik of Denmark." They were married over 50 years till he died in 2018. She gave birth to a son Prince Frederik and a year later had a second child Joachim in 1969. Frederick found his bride in Australia. Margrethe is an accomplished painter and held many arts shows over the years. She has been a chain smoker and is well known for her tobacco habit and announced in 2006, she would only smoke in private. She struggled with many health issues and endured several operations.

Mary, Crown Princess of Denmark

(466)

Mary Donaldson was born 5 February, 1972 in Tasmania Australia, the youngest of 4 children, the family was Scottish. In school she loved sports, played basketball, hockey, and studied music, played piano, flute, and clarinet. In 1974 the family lived in Texas where she started school at Clear Lake City Elementary in Houston. In 1975 they moved to Tasmania, Australia; there she went to Hobart College and studied at the University of Tasmania graduating in 1996 with a combined Bachelor of Commerce and Bachelor of Laws and qualified with certificates in Advertising Federation of Australia (AFA) and direct marketing from the Australian Direct Marketing Association (ADMA). Her mother died from complications following heart surgery in 1997 when Mary was 25. A few years later her father married British Author and novelist Susan Moody. She studied French and worked briefly as a tutor in Paris. Mary met Crown Prince Frederik of Denmark at the Slip Inn on 16 Sept. 2000 during the Summer Olympics in Sydney, and conducted a long-distance relationship; at first she did not know he was the Crown Prince of Denmark, which was a pleasant surprise when she discovered that. Frederik made a number of discreet visits to Australia, On 15 Nov. 2001 the Danish magazine *Billed Bladet* named Mary as Frederik's girlfriend; after that she moved from Australia to Denmark. In Sept. 2003 the Danish court announced that his mother Queen Margrethe II intended to give her consent to the marriage at the State Council meeting on 8 October, 2003 at which time the couple became officially engaged. From then on Mary's main priority was to become fluent in the Danish language. She acknowledged in media interviews that this was a major challenge for her. (Both Lana & Terry, are European and can testify to the fact that it takes a lot of effort to become fluent in another language). Mary & Frederik married on 14 May 2004 in Copenhagen Cathedral, and spent their honeymoon in Africa. The marriage is blest with 4 children: Prince Christian born 15 Oct. 2005, Princess Isabella born 21 April 2007, and the twins Prince Vincent & Princess Josephine both born 8 Jan. 2011. All four have many more names but our space here is limited. The Danish Parliament passed a special law: (*Mary's Law*), giving her Danish citizenship upon marriage, (a standard procedure for new foreign members of the royal family), before that she was a dual citizen of Australia and the United Kingdom. Mary had been a Presbyterian and converted to the Evangelical Lutheran Church upon her marriage. She is active in the Home Guard and has a working relationship with numerous charities. Mary Foundation was formed to combat Bullying & Domestic Violence.

Brother Andrew

(467)

Andrew van der Bijl was born 11 May 1928 in Alkmaar, in the Netherlands. In 1946 he enlisted in the Army and was posted to Indonesia; there he was shot twice in the foot, and upon he returning home in 1949 found himself convalescing in the care of Christian nurses, one of them being Corrie van Dam, married her, and they have 5 children. He was invited to a revival meeting where he embraced the Christian faith and began Evangelistic Crusade Missionary Training College in Glasgow, taking Bible classes on *systematic theology*, *linguistics*, and *car mechanics*. The students were sent into Scotland in groups of five with only 1 pound each (about US $1.14), with that were to pay for transport, lodgings, and food. They were not to ask for monetary needs on their travels, but were expected to refund the 1 pound after 30 days, and discovered they had more than needed. Andrew returned enough money to send all the students on worldwide missions. That 3-year training got him started in mission work lasting 60 years in more than 125 countries while serving the global church as God's Smuggler visiting places that banned Bibles, all countries behind the Iron Curtain in his blue Volkswagen Beetle bringing Bibles where the sacred book was banned. He became known as "God's Smuggler" slipping past border guards with Bibles bulging in every space of that little car. As he reached the checkpoints with his VW filled with Bibles that were banned in all these countries, he prayed this prayer at every border crossing: "*Lord, in my luggage I have scriptures I want to take to your children; when You were on earth, You made blind eyes see; now I pray make seeing eyes blind. Do not let the guards see those things You don't want them to see.*" In 1967 he wrote the book titled *God's Smuggler*, filled with stories about getting past those guards. The book has been printed in 35 languages and sold over 10 million copies, and has inspired millions. He said: don't ask God to remove persecution; it's the seed of the Christian Faith. He founded Open Doors Ministries, now focused more on Islam, although his early ministry was centered on Communist countries; and began with going to a youth conference in Poland, there he snuck away from the group to visit some secret believers distributing tracts entitled: "*The way of Salvation*." Upon returning home people began supporting his ministry. He had started in Poland, then visited Albania, Lebanon, Uganda, China, Cuba, and after demise of the Soviet Union set his sights on the next threat, which is Islam. He wrote 16 more books, and died 27 Sept. in the Netherlands at age 94 and may well have been one of the greatest missionaries of all time. Brother Andrew died on 27 September, 2022.

Tulsi Gabbard

(468)

Tulsi Gabbard was born 12 April 1981 in American Samoa, and is the fourth of five children born to Mike & Carol Gabbard. We have not met Tulsi as an adult but have been close to her parents. Her mother Carol is Caucasian and her father Mike is European-Samoan, meaning Tulsi was raised, (*like many in Hawaii*), in a multicultural family. She was home schooled, except for two years at an all-girls school in the Philippines. we learned about her father through his radio program "<u>*Let's talk straight Hawaii,*</u>" and discovered he was the owner of "<u>Down to Earth</u>" on King St. & hold similar political views on many issues, & decided to increase patronizing his business; it was not hard to do as it was an all vegetarian store that suited much of our food requirements, <u>*and*</u> we were both small business owners. Mike & Carol have been in our home in Hawaii Kai, and have always admired the family. His personal cell nr is still on my phone. We have a long standing agreement; if & when Tulsi comes home, I would like to take her to lunch, or at minimum share a cappuccino. Mike & I served for several years on the same political committees, and it was disappointing (told him so), when he signed on to the Democratic Party, but our friendship was never affected. For Tulsi the home state is now enemy territory & with security issues, meeting her may get relegated to the wish list. Tulsi has kissed her good-buys to the Democratic Party and has publicly expressed <u>some</u> of the following reasons: "She left because the Democratic Party is now under complete control of an elitist cabal of warmongers driven by cowardly wokeness, and are dividing the country by racializing every issue, stoking anti-white racism and actively working to undermine our God-given freedoms enshrined in the Constitution, they are hostile to people of faith and spirituality. They demonize the police and protect the criminals at the expense of law-abiding Americans. They believe in open borders and weaponize the national security state to go after political opponents. Above all else, the Democrats of today are dragging us ever closer to nuclear war. They are the Party that stands for a government <u>of</u>, <u>by</u>, and <u>for</u>, the powerful elite." Tulsi expressed these reasons for her exit, and that qualified her to appear here; it's our hope that Mike (who is not a Democrat by conviction), will do the same. Tulsi first served in the Haw. State House of Representatives & was deployed to Iraq with the Hawaii Army National Guard, then served in Kuwait, after that was elected to the US House of Repr., She criticized the Obama administration for refusing to identify radical Islam & their extremism as the real enemy. She ran for President but decided to endorse Biden, but that never stopped Tulsi from expressing her convictions. We often wondered: "How long will the Democrats keep her?"

Everett Dirksen

(469)

Everett McKinley Dirksen was born 4 January, 1896 in Pekin Illinois. His parents were German immigrants who came from East Frisia. The families were strong Republicans even naming their son after the leading candidate for the Presidential nomination at that time. Obviously, they had strong political leanings, and Everett demonstrated the same when serving in uniform. He dropped out of college on his 21st birthday in 1917, and joined the US Army; 3 months later the US entered WW-1, and he was deployed to France, commissioned as a 2nd lieutenant. Due to his fluent German the Army tried to keep him but he had other goals and could do more on the outside. He invested in a failing venture of an electric washing machine business; after that joined other family members in the Dirksen Brothers Bakery and tried writing while working at various city political positions. He ran unsuccessfully for a US House position, but on 2nd attempt secured a seat. He later went to the US Senate where he had a successful legislative career. In 1966 introduced a constitutional amendment to permit student led prayers in public schools; it gained only 49 of the required 67 votes needed. Regarding the Vietnam War he said I have been there 3 times, it costs us $1.5 million a day, there are 15,500 troops there, even though we are not supposed to have combatant troops on the ground, but will have to muddle through it to see what we can do and although I agree with the goals of the Johnson administration about Vietnam, but vigorously criticize their prosecution of the war. He was a talented orator with his notably deep rich baritone voice while talking slow he delivered some flamboyant speeches on the Senate floor that would compel you to stop and listen. It caused people to refer to him as "*The Wizard of Ooze*." When he first came, he said there are 100 personalities here, what an amazing thing it is to harmonize them. He was notorious for holding the line on excessive spending, and upon studying the finances connected to the many legislative bills the Senate was considering for passage; Senator Dirksen would rise to his feet and got every one's attention when he said: "*A billion here and a billion there, and pretty soon you're talking some real money*." (if he was there today the Billion would likely change to Trillion.) On Sept. 7, 1969 Everett Dirksen suffered a cardiac arrest and died at age 73. His body was laid in state at the US Capitol rotunda, followed by burial at Pekin Illinois. When political discussions became tense he would lighten the atmosphere by taking up his perennial campaign to have the Marigold named as the national flower, it never succeeded. A statue of him stands on the grounds of the State Capitol in Springfield Illinois; and a US senate office building has been named after him. He was a rare statesman.

Gladys West

(470)

Gladys Mae West Brown was born on October 27, 1930 in Sutherland, rural county south of Richmond Virginia. Family was African-American in community of sharecroppers, and she spent her childhood working on small family farm. Mother worked in tobacco factory & father was farmer, also worked for the railroad to help support the family. Gladys decided early in life she did not want to work in the tobacco fields or factories and knew her only way out was to get an education, but that was expensive, therefore the big obstacle was finance; she began babysitting but that did not go far for the education she was hoping for. Not expecting this in high school her superior academic performance resulted in securing two scholarships to Virginia State University, historically a black school. She graduated Valedictorian in 1948, having excelled in all topics; she chose mathematics, (a field mostly occupied by men), and graduated with a Bachelor of Science; became a member of the Alpha Kappa Alpha sorority. She taught science and math for 2 years until West was hired in 1956 at the Naval Proving ground (now called <u>Naval Surface Warfare Center</u>). She was the 2nd black woman ever hired, and earned a 2nd master's degree in public administration from the University of Oklahoma. In 1960 she participated in an award-winning astronomical study that proved the regularity of Pluto's motion relative to Neptune. Due to her keen technological ability and superior intellect, became project manager for the Seasat radar altimetry project, the first satellite that could remotely sense oceans, cut her teams processing time in half & was recommended for a commendation in 1979. By mid-1980's she programmed an IBM 7030 Stretch Computer to deliver increasingly precise calculations to model the shape of the earth; an ellipsoid with additional undulations known as the *geoid*. Generating an extremely accurate geopotential model required her to employ complex algorithms to account for variations in gravitational tidal and other forces that distort Earth's shape. In her autobiography, West spoke of the complex problems she solved, which had proven too difficult for other members of the team. Some of her technological discoveries were published in a 51-page technical report from The Naval Surface Weapons Center (NSWC); published to increase accuracy of the estimation of geoid heights & vertical deflection, important for satellite geodesy. West retired after working 42 years, and instead of resting, she completed a Ph.D. in Public Administration from Virginia Tech. In 2018 she was inducted in the US Air Force Hall of Fame. Her mathematical discoveries are far too numerous to list here.

Constantine the Great

(471)

Flavius Valerius Constantinus was born about 27 February 272 in Naissus, Moesia in the Roman Empire, (now Serbia). He was the son of an esteemed Roman army officer; his mother was a Greek Christian lady of low birth. He was educated in Latin, Literature, and Greek Philosophy, and was able to mix well within the intelligentsia circles of his day. He became a Roman Emperor in 306 at his young age of 34. Although he had lived much of his life as a pagan, Constantine was the first Roman Emperor to convert to Christianity, and had a positive role in the proclamation of the edict of Milan in 313AD which declared tolerance for Christians in the Roman Empire. The Church of the Holy Sepulcher was built on his orders; it was deemed to be the site of Jesus tomb in Jerusalem considered to be one of the most holy places in Christendom. The medieval church held up Constantine as a paragon of virtue while secular rulers invoked him as a prototype and cymbal of imperial legitimacy. He was very different from dictators such Julius Cesar before him & Nero, who ruled while Rome burned. Constantine built the imperial residence in the city of Byzantium which was renamed Constantinople after his name, (now Istanbul); it became the capital of the empire for more than a thousand years. Constantine was a ruler of major importance although he has always been a controversial figure; historians with anti-Christian bias have spread much misinformation about him, although he was over 40 when he finally declared himself a Christian making it clear that he owed all his successes to God alone. The African Bishops asked him to intervene in some disputes; prompting him to call 150 mostly Eastern Bishops and learned man and convoked the first Council of Constantinople in 325 AD which resulted also in the <u>Nicene Creed</u>, still honored today by the majority of Christendom throughout the world (discussed on another page in this book). Constantine enacted new laws making it illegal for Jews to seek converts or bring Jews back who had converted to Christianity, and Jews were forbidden to own Christian slaves. In the year 337 Constantine fell seriously ill, and left Constantinople for the hot baths near his mother's city of Helenopolis. In a church his mother built he prayed while he was dying telling the bishops of his wish to be baptized in the River Jordan where Christ was baptized. Seeing how sick he was he got immediate action, and chose Bishop Eusebius of Nicomedia to perform the ceremony. He died soon after on <u>22 May, 337</u> at age 65 in Achyron Roman Empire, (now Turkey). <u>Nis Constantine the Great Airport</u> is named in his honor as well as numerous churches and cathedrals throughout the world. The name Constantine enjoyed renewed popularity for 12 centuries.

John Wesley
(472)

John Wesley was born 28 June 1703 in Epworth, Lincolnshire, England. He nearly lost his life when at age 5 in a rectory fire he was rescued from the 2nd floor and lifted out of the window by a man standing on another man's shoulders. He was educated at Charterhouse and attended Christ Church in Oxford. He was ordained in 1726 and became an Anglican priest. He led the "*Holy Club*" society founded by his brother Charles with members such as George Whitefield; the club aimed to pursue a devout Christian life; and met daily for 3 hours of prayer, learning the Psalms, and read from the Greek Testament, visited prisoners, and cared for the sick; some considered them religious fanatics. Wesley and Whitefield preached outdoors, quite new for the Church of England. In contrast to Whitefield's Calvinism, Wesley embraced Armenian doctrines. His followers were called Methodists; he organized small groups and appointed unordained itinerant Evangelists, both women and men to care for these groups involving themselves in the social issues of the day such as abolition of slavery, prison reform & others. Although he was not a systematic theologian he argued for Christian perfection and opposed Calvinism who taught the doctrine of predestination. After an unsuccessful ministry of 2 years, he returned to London and in 1738 joined the Moravian

Christians, and learned from them about genuine Evangelical conversion. He had met them on one of those voyages to the new world where the ship experienced a major storm and the mast broke; Wesley was terrified thinking the ship was going down; but the Moravians were singing and possessed inner peace and strength Wesley did not have. Although he remained within the established Church of England, they were barred from preaching in many parish churches even though the brothers were ordained there, but the church persecuted Methodists. Wesley had begun ministering in the new world in Savannah Georgia. After meeting the Moravians his preaching changed and he began to call sinners to repent and follow Christ, which was not done in the main church. His sermons became foreign to the established church. The fact that He was barred from most churches became a blessing, when they preached in the parks their audience was often between 10,000 and 50.000; there was no church in all of England that could accommodate that many. When his health began to decline, Wesley stopped preaching; on 2 March 1791 he died at age 87 leaving behind 135,000 members, 541 itinerant preachers, and a new denomination called Methodist, many schools and a university. In 2002 (over 200 years after his death), he was listed #50 on BBC's list of 100 greatest Britons.

Marcus Aurelius

(473)

Marcus Aurelius Antoninus was born 26 April 121 in Rome during the reign of Roman Emperor Hadrian. His father died when he was three resulting in his mother & grandfather raising him. After Hadrian's son Aelius Caesar died, the emperor adopted Marcus's Uncle Antoninus Pius in 138 as his new heir. In turn Antoninus adopted Marcus and Lucius, the son of Aelius. Marcus's mother Domitia Lucilla Minor was from a very wealthy family. She inherited a great fortune from her parents and grandparents, which included large brickworks on the outskirts of Rome. When Hadrian died, Antoninus became emperor, and Marcus Aurelius became heir to the throne; he studied Greek and Latin under tutors such as Herodes Atticus and Marcus Cornelius Fronto. He married Antoninus's daughter Faustina in 145 at age 24. After Antoninus died in 161, Marcus Aurelius acceded to the throne alongside his adoptive brother, who reigned under the name Lucius Verus. Under his rule the empire witnessed heavy military conflict, but Marcus defeated the Marcomanni, Quadi, and Sarmatian Iazyges in the Marcomanni wars; however, these and other Germanic influence began to represent a troubling reality for the empire. He modified the silver purity of the Roman currency <u>*the denarius*</u>. Some historians have claimed that the persecution of Christians increased during his reign but that does not balance with other facts; because it was Tertulian who called Marcus a protector of Christians. In 165, The Antonine Plague (*aka the Galen Plague named after the physician who described it*), broke out and devastated the Roman Empire inhabitants causing the death of 5 to 10 million people, (about 25% of the population), and Lucius Verus may have died from that plague in 169; plagues are no respecter of persons. Marcus had chosen not to adopt an heir; his children included Lucilla, who married Lucius, and Commodus, succession after Marcus has been subject of much debate. The life of Marcus Aurelius is somewhat patchy and a little unreliable; the reason for that was that the historical writers differed about what happened. In the early days there may not have been a great concern to ascertain actual historical data, subsequently there are various versions written about what actually happened in antiquity, and we have no way to certify its accuracy. Having said that historians seem to have agreed to the fact that Marcus Aurelius was the last of the *good emperors* that ruled during a time when there was relative peace and stability in the Roman Empire from 27 BC to 180 AD. Marcus was beloved by the people of Rome; and was a popular emperor. He died at age 58 on 17 March 180, his spouse Faustina had died 5 years earlier.

Johann Sebastian Bach

(474)

Johann Sebastian Bach was born 21 March, 1685 in Eisenach, Germany, and was the 8th and youngest child in the musical Bach family. Eisenach is where Germany & Hungary settled their bitter disputes in the wars of 908; it was where Martin Luther spent his childhood years, and Napoleon who came about 100 years after Bach and fought some of his battles there meaning this city experienced turbulent times especially during the Reformation years of the 16th century, and Bach grew up in a town filled with rich history much of it with many troubling years of controversy before & after him it was also the domicile of people who just like Bach made great improvements on the world. Johann lost his mother and father before he was ten, although his father likely taught him organ, violin, and basic music; he gave him a clavichord at a young age, and also learned music from his older brother. The family had already produced several composers when he was born. At age ten he began to live with his eldest brother till 1703. Up to that time he was primarily composing organ music, as well as the well-tempered clavier always appreciated for its didactic qualities. He worked as musician mostly in protestant churches. (in 1948 when *I was 13, my cousins took me to a concert of Bach Organ Music in one of the large churches in Den Haag where Albert Schweitzer played that enormous pipe organ, to raise funds for his leper colony in Africa; after the program we met Schweitzer and I purchased one of his 33lp records of Bach music by Schweitzer and played it over & over, even though the music was over my head at the time, but by owning that record, I began to develop a love for the Bach organ music.*) Bach received instruction in Theology, Latin and Greek, at the local gymnasium. In 1703 he became the organist in Arnstadt with light duties for a small, but generous salary. He was dissatisfied with the choir and left for Buxtehude walking the 450 Kilometer of foot. In 1706 he received the post as organist at the Blasius church for increased remuneration, improved living, and a better choir; the church renovated the organ, and there he married Maria Barbara Bach his 2nd cousin. In 1708 he worked as konzertmeister at the ducal court where he worked with well-funded musicians, at a time when their first baby was born. Later his eyes deteriorated and the British eye surgeon that treated him was a charlatan and blinded Bach. He died on 28 July 1750 at age 65 in Leipzig, from complications due to incompetent medical treatment. 200 years later in 1950 Wolfgang Schmieder published a *Bach works Catalogue* listing *1080* of Bach's compositions, he was a musical genius.

Wolfgang Amadeus Mozart

(475)

Wolfgang Amadeus Mozart was born on 27 January 1756, to Leopold Mozart & Anna Maria Pertl in Salzburg, a Principality in the Holy Roman Empire, (now Austria). He was the youngest of 7 children, 5 of whom died in infancy. He composed at age 5 and played it to his father, although scholars have argued if he was composing as young as age 4. In the early years his father was his only teacher instructing him in music, languages, and academic topics. (Today such tasks are mostly relegated to the schools but in antiquity the home was the primary place to get educated). His first ink-spattered composition surprised his father who gave up on composing when it was evident that his son's musical talents may have surpassed his own. At a young age the family toured Europe, doing more than sightseeing, beginning with a exhibition in 1762 at the court of prince-elector Maximilian III of Bavaria in Munich; then onto the Imperial Courts in Vienna and Prague followed by a three and a half year tour to the courts of Mannheim, Paris, Dover, The Hague, Amsterdam, Utrecht, London and Zurich. During that trip Wolfgang met renowned musicians and composers. Of particular significance was a visit in London with Johann Christian Bach at age of 8. It was at that age he wrote his first symphony. The family trips were very challenging as travel conditions were most primitive. They had to wait for invitations and reimbursement from nobility, while waiting they endured long, near fatal illnesses when far from home. After one year at home in Salzburg Wolfgang set out with only his father for a one-and-a-half-year tour of Italy. On that tour he met Josef Mislivecek & Giovanni Battista Martini in Bologna and was accepted as a member of the famous Accademia Filarmonica. Then he met the emperor, who eventually supported his career with commissions and a part time position. In 1781 he had established himself as the finest keyboard player in Vienna. His music career fared better than his courtships; he was not able to win the hand of Aloysia Weber, but later had a little more success with her sister Constanze, although the more challenging task was to get his father's permission which finally came, and the couple were married on 4 August 1782. Some have suggested that a much slower output of music was the result of suffering from depression. In 1791 he fell ill and on 5 December 1791 at age 35 he died. Ludwig Van Beethoven (15 years his junior) was deeply influenced by his work. Wolfgang Amadeus Mozart is widely regarded as one of the greatest composers in the history of Western music, admired for its melodic beauty, its formal elegance and richness of harmony and texture.

Joseph Haydn

(476)

Franz Joseph Haydn was born on 31 March 1732 in Rohrau Austria, his father served as a village mayor, his mother Maria Koller had worked as a cook in the palace of Count Harrach, who was the presiding aristocrat. Neither parent could read music, however Mathias was an enthusiastic folk musician who had taught himself to play the harp, and the Haydn family would often sing with the neighbors, (very common in Europe). People soon noticed that young Joseph was musically gifted and suggested that he take training. When he was age 6 they accepted a proposal from the schoolmaster and the choirmaster for Joseph be apprenticed to Frankh in his home to train as a musician, and young Joseph went with him to Hainburg (a picturesque town in Hesse Germany on the banks of the Danube River). After that he never lived again with his parents. Living with Frankh was not easy he was frequently hungry, and humiliated by the filthy state of his clothing, but immersed himself in training and soon could play harpsichord & violin. The people of Hainburg heard him sing treble parts in the church choir. In 1739 he came to the attention of Georg von Reutter the director of music in St Stephen's Cathedral in Vienna who was looking for choirboys and took him to Vienna in 1740 where he worked for the next 9 years as a chorister while living with the Reutter family along with four other choirboys, one of them was his younger brother Michael. The choirboys were instructed in Latin, Voice, Violin, and Keyboard. St Steven's was one of the leading musical centers in Europe, he learned much there. His reputation increased and he eventually obtained aristocratic patronage, crucial for the career of a composer in his day. Countess Thun had seen one of Haydn's compositions, and summoned him as her singing & keyboard instructor. In 1756 Baron Carl Josef Furnberg employed Haydn at his country estate Weinzierl. There he did more writing, which became a turning point in his career. He was in great demand as a performer and teacher, earning 200 florins a year plus free board. In 1760 with the security of a Kapellmeister position at age 28 he married Maria Anna Theresia Keller, although had previously been in love with her sister. The marriage produced no children, was most unhappy, and both took lovers. In later years his health declined to the point that he was not able to compose, became weak & dizzy. When his career was winding down, he found solace sitting at the piano. On 26 May he played the "Emperor's Hymn" with unusual gusto and 5 days later on 31 May 1809 at age 77 he peacefully died in his home, he was a devout Catholic. As a musician he excelled in every musical genre and composed 107 symphonies.

Giuseppe Verdi

(477)

Giuseppe Fortunino Francesco Verdi was born 9 or 10 October 1813 in Italy, the first child of Carlo Verdi & Luigia Uttini, (days began at sunset therefore the date is in dispute but he celebrated his own birthday on 9 October). His younger sister died at age 17, she was his closest friend. From age 4 he was privately tutored in Latin and Italian by the schoolmaster Baistrocci and at age 6 he attended the village school. After learning to play the organ he showed so much interest, his parents gave him a spinet, and provided organ lessons; at age 8 Verdi became the official paid organist at the local church. The family was literate but could not read music. At age 10 he was enrolled in Busseto school for boys and later went on to the gymnasia walking there a great distance on foot. At age 11 he was schooled in Italian, the Humanities, Latin, and Rhetoric; at 12 he received lessons in music from Ferdinando Provesi (director of the municipal music school). At 13 he graduated from the Ginnasio with honors, after that devote all his time to music and from 13-18 he wrote an assortment pieces of band and march music and played in the local philharmonic orchestra, there he established himself as a leader, the secretary of the organization wrote; "*no one could rival him*", he showed vivid imagination in the arrangement of instrumental parts, but Verdi had set his sights on Milan, the cultural capital of northern Italy, he applied to study at the conservatory but was not accepted. The years from 1851 to 1853 were filled with operatic activity; he and Giusepponi visited Paris, and there he was inspired to compose La Traviata. In our family he has always been one of the greatest composers surpassing all others even though he may not have risen to the level of Bach & Beethoven, but music is all a matter of personal taste. In 1872 he spent a lot of his time on the production of _Aida_ at Milan & Naples, _which was my personal favorite,_ especially that _triumphal march_ in to Egypt listening to the trumpets we could vividly see the march in our imagination and played the music 10,000 times, we did not have the money to see the opera but could see it clearly in our imagination. It is an opera in 4 parts set in the old kingdom of Egypt; what always fascinated me that a man who lived in the early part of the 19th century had so much imagination. Aida still holds a central place in the operatic canon receiving performances every year around the world. At New York's Metropolitan opera, Aida has been sung more than 1,100 times. In 1901 Giuseppe Verdi suffered a stroke, and on 27 January he died at age 87; is crediting with writing 32 Operas and many other musical pieces, in our opinion he was one of the greatest composers who ever lived, with Aida & La Traviata being the crown jewels of his career.

Ngozi Fulani

(478)

Ngozi Fulani is a special lady and should be on these pages. She was born & raised in Britain, although her parents moved there from Barbados. We visited Barbados in 1957, it is an island country, and was a British colony; we were told that of the inhabitants, mostly are descendants of the slave trade until it was outlawed by the Slavery Abolition act of 1833. When we visited there, the local people were hoping to become independent soon, and indeed self-governing came in 1966; the population is predominantly of African ancestry. Barbados is technically an Atlantic Island but it is closely associated with the Caribbean. We were told at one time in about 1660 there were 27,000 Nigerian black slaves living on Barbados, which was the peak of the sugar plantation days. Our visit was a little disappointing; it was not what we had expected to find in a Caribbean island, it was raining and the streets were muddy. We have not been back, but it is our understanding that after the independence of 1966 its infrastructure has been substantially upgraded making it now a leading tourist destination. Ngozi Fulani's parents had moved out of Barbados to England before she was born in Britain, was educated in Hackney east London and there she learned the Emashi dance celebrating African arts & culture. During that time, she met *(now King)* Charles.

In 2015 Fulani saw a need and founded the charity *Sistah Space*, which provides support and refuge for women and girls of African and Caribbean heritage who have experienced domestic abuse in England. The organization has worked with amazing success and became much more than a charity on paper, it was publicly recognized for its U.K work with abused ladies. Her work got the attention of Buckingham Palace and she was invited to a reception honoring her as a leading figure working with abused victims to raise awareness of the issues surrounding violence against women & girls. That reception was attended by Queen Rania of Jordan, Queen Mathilda of Belgium, Crown princess Mary of Denmark, and Olena Zelensky of Ukraine as well as a whole string royals close to Buckingham Palace. This found her in some very prestigious company and recounted that at that reception racially insensitive remarks were made inferring she is from some backward African country rather than honoring her as a lady born & raised in England who helped many. One Royal lady asked her repeatedly: *what part of Africa are u from? Where in Africa are u born?* Fulani kept on saying I was born here in England, but it did not satisfy the lady. When this became known, the royal family was embarrassed about such insensitive remarks, (at least now Meghan Markle will feel vindicated). It may be wise to educate the Royals about the far reaching British Empire. We believe Fulani saw a need and did something about it; she made a difference.

Frederic Chopin
(479)

Frederic Franciszek Chopin was born March 1, 1810 in Zelazowa, Warsaw Poland. His father Nicolas Chopin was a Frenchman and his mother was Justyna Krzyzanofska. He wrote music and is known for his professional technique, so much so, that he is without equal in his generation. He may have had some piano instruction from his mother, but his first professional music tutor from 1816 to 1821 was the Czech pianist Wojciech Zywny and occasionally played duets with her brother, at age 7 he began giving public concerts and wrote two polonaises in G minor and B flat major. Chopin's successes as a composer and performer opened the door to Western Europe for him and he settled in Paris; there he formed a friendship with Franz Liszt and Robert Schumann. In 1830 he returned to Warsaw but had wanted to go to Italy; due to violent unrest there Italy was too dangerous at that time and his next choice was living in Paris; he arrived there 5 October 1831 and never returned to Warsaw. In Paris he was introduced to the piano manufacturer Camille Pleyel. This was the beginning of a long and close association between the composer and Pleyel's instruments. After a failed engagement to Maria Wodzinska he maintained an often troubled relationship with French writer Aurore Dupin (known by her pen name George Sand). All of Chopin's compositions include the piano; most are for solo piano, though he also wrote two piano concertos, a few chamber pieces and some set to Polish lyrics. His piano writing was technically demanding and expanded the limits of the instrument. In his final years he was supported financially by his admirer Jane Stirling, who also arranged for him to visit Scotland in 1848. Chopin's music, his status as one of music's earliest celebrities, and his early death, has made him a leading symbol of the Romantic era and his works remain popular today. But from 1842 onwards Chopin showed signs of serious illness. After a solo recital in Paris he wrote I have to lie in bed all day my tonsils are aching so much, and from then on he was forced to decline many invitations for recitals. With his health further deteriorating Chopin desired to have a family member with him and his sister Ludwika came to Paris with her husband & daughter. Chopin made his last public appearance on a concert platform at London's Guildhall on 16 November 1848 where he played a benefit for the Polish refugees. He was now seriously ill and it became evident that his illness was terminal. For most of his life, Chopin was in poor health, and he died in Paris in 1849 at age 39, probably of pericarditis which was likely aggravated by tuberculosis. Over 230 works of Chopin survive. All his known works are mostly piano concertos, & songs for chamber music.

Theodore Beza

(480)

Theodore Beza was born on 24 June 1519 in France, his mother died when he was three, and his uncle saw to it that he got a good education and enrolled him at Orleans in Paris; there he studied under Melchior Wolmar who taught him Greek & Latin. He graduated at age 20 with a degree in civil law fully intending to practice in Paris, but got very sick and discovered the literature of the Reformers. The church offered him no assurance and he cried out to God asking for truth. He received substantial support from the church, although in his heart he was protestant but hesitated to leave the church that had helped him, and was vacillating whether he should stay in, or join the Reformers, he and his wife moved to Geneva. The church saw a man of great learning and sent skilled debaters to Geneva to win him back in the fold but he stood firm. He examined why Luther had not made a total break with Catholic teaching, when it concerned the Lords-Supper that it was the real body & blood of Christ. Calvin & Beza said it was a Feast of Remembrance. The Lords supper that we celebrate today in most protestant circles is based on the teaching and writings of Beza which he summarized in his book titled "<u>The Conciliatone</u>;" in there he clarified the meaning of: <u>this is my body and my blood</u>. Sadly, Luther and Calvin never came to agreement on that issue. Those of us who are members in general protestant churches today, when we celebrate *Holy Communion*; we are practicing the teaching of Theodore Beza who was a French Protestant, Scholar, Theologian, Reformer, as well as being a disciple of John Calvin, living much of his life in Geneva, working diligently for the cause of the Reformation. He was a model pastor and theologian who had deep love and affection for his people, (we who live in the Western world in the 21st century may never fully comprehend the meaning of that, while Huguenots who lived after the St Bartholomew massacre which was inflicted on Protestants called Huguenots by the church). Beza loved his parishioners, even interceded for them in the courts. He served for 7 months with the Huguenot army, and performed the funeral for his dear friend John Calvin. At that time a commitment to Christ might cost your life, and indeed many were massacred by the bloodthirsty priests and bishops who were soldiers for their King and were sure Christ would want them to do that. Beza broke with all Catholic traditions and made a difference to millions; he worked for the Reformation till the day he died at age 86 on October 13, 1605. He had a real pastoral heart with vision, and was willing to pay the prize, which many of his followers paid. We had only learned about him in school but was deeply moved when I came face to face with the monument on the Reformation Wall at the university of Geneva, I went back 3 more times.

Hans Egede

(481)

Hans Poulsen Egede was born 31 Jan. 1686 in Harstad, Denmark (north of the Arctic Circle). His grandfather had been a vicar in Denmark; Hans was schooled by an uncle, a clergyman in the Lutheran Church. In 1704 he went to the University of Copenhagen and earned a Bachelor's degree in Theology; in 1707 he married Gertrud Rasch who was 13 years his senior. They went to Greenland in 1721 and found no Europeans there; the Island was primarily occupied by <u>*Eskimos or Inuit*</u>; (a group of culturally similar indigenous people who are inhabitants of the Arctic Regions, such as Greenland, Labrador, Northern Canada, Alaska and other territories in the far north), he has been credited with revitalizing the Dano-Norwegian interest in the Island which had been lost for about 300 years, although the name Greenland seems inappropriate for an island that is 85% covered in ice, snow, and arctic glaciers, (<u>*perhaps it should trade names with Iceland*</u>). He established the Capital Godthab (now known as Nuuk). The island is geographically part of North America but is culturally, linguistically, and politically more connected to Europe. Egede became the equivalent of a national saint of Greenland, and the town of Egedesminde commemorates him, which was established by his 2nd son Niels in 1759, on the Eqalussuit peninsula, it was the site of the pre-Viking Inuit settlement. A grandson and namesake also worked in the island as a missionary and published a celebrated diary highlighting his time there. Hans's celebrity status reached far beyond Greenland. The Egede crater on the south edge of the Mare Frigoris (*the Sea of Gold*) on the moon is named in his honor. Fishing and Whaling are the major industries in Greenland. What is unique about Greenland? There are no roads on the island that connect towns, except air travel. The land is 2.1 million sq miles, making it the largest Island in the world with 56000 people, of which 17000 of them live in the capital; the language is mostly Danish although English is commonly understood. The island was a Danish colony till 1953. During WW-II, by joint agreement, defense was handled by the US. Statues of Hans Egede stand watch over Greenland's capital; one is in Nuuk as well as one outside Frederik's church in Copenhagen. The monument was vandalized with the word "*decolonize*" spray painted on its base during worldwide protests against memorials of colonial figures, another Egede statue in Nuuk was likewise vandalized in response the Danish parliament voted 921 to 600 to keep the statue. Some have called Hans Egede the Apostle of Greenland. He died at 72 on 5 Nov. 1758.

Briet Bjarnhedinsdottir
(482)

Although I grew up tri-lingual and never had problems with Japanese or Chinese names, even could handle the 85 letter Maori place name back in NZ, thinking it was the world's longest name until we saw that Thailand has a 168 letter town; but please don't ask me to pronounce this one. Briet was born 27 Sept. 1856 in Iceland and at age 24 she was faced with the fact that girls were not given the opportunity to receive further education. At age 16 she had written an article about the Status of Women but did not show it to anyone till 13 years later, then published it in 1885 under the pseudonym Esa. In 1887 she moved to Reykjavik and the following year married Valdimar Asmundsson, but in 1902 he died suddenly, together they had 2 children. In 1894 she was one of the founders of the Icelandic Women's Society and in 1895 began publishing the Women's newspaper serving as editor till 1926; in 1898 she published the Children's newspaper. Briet could identify with her readers and traveled around Denmark, Norway, and Sweden. She met Carrie Chapman Catt who had founded The International Woman Suffrage Alliance and invited her to the first Congress of the International Suffrage Association in Berlin in 1904. Catt was elected Chairman and invited Briet to the 1906 meeting in Copenhagen. There were no women's organizations in

Iceland yet and she became the founder of the first Icelandic Women's Rights Association, was elected chairman from 1907 till 1911 and again from 1912 to 1927. Then several Icelandic Women's organizations merged and wanted her leadership qualities. She befriended Mayor Knud Zimsen and in 1912 together they sponsored a steam-roller which was a prerequisite for paving the streets of Reykjavik considered to be a major improvement for the city. After the device arrived some of the town councilors thought it be best to call the machine Briet/Knutsdottir, but in the end it became *Briet*; when people saw the machine working in the city, they would always think of her. The device faithfully paved all the city streets and retired in January 2008, after that it was displayed at the Reykjavik City Hall as an exhibition to memorialize the major accomplishments of the women's movement in Iceland. Briet was awarded the Knights Cross of the Icelandic Falcon in 1928 and was the first named woman to have her picture on a stamp in Iceland in 1978. Three city streets were named after her. In 1914 she was listed as number four on the national list of leaders. On 16 March 1940 she died at age 84 in Reykjavik. On Women's Rights day 19 June 2011 her memory was formally honored by the city of Reykjavik, she made a difference for women around the world.

Vigdis Finnbogadottir

(483)

Vigdis was born 15 April, 1930 in Reykjavik in the kingdom of Iceland. Her father was a professor and a civil engineer and her mother was a nurse, as well as the chairperson of the Icelandic Nurses Association. Together her parents had 2 children. After passing her matriculation exam in 1949, Vigdis studied French, and French Literature, at the University of Grenoble, (<u>*a major scientific center in the field of computer science and applied mathematics, at the Sorbonne in Paris*</u>), from 1949 to 1953; after that she studied the history of theater at the University of Copenhagen. Then acquired a BA in French & English as well as a Professional Graduate Certificate in Education at the University of Iceland, She married a physician in 1954 but the marriage did not work out and divorced 9 years later in 1963. At age 41 Vigdis adopted a daughter, becoming the first single woman in Iceland to be allowed to adopt a child. She did not support the US military presence in Iceland and participated in some protests expressing that, sometimes even joined the 50 km walk that was held once a year. After graduating she taught French drama at the University and experimental theatre. From 1954 to 1957, and again from 1961 to 1964 she worked with the Reykjavik Theatre Company on experimental bases. During the summers she worked as a tour guide. That exposed her to the International community and her linguistic abilities were very helpful, especially when the French & Swiss groups came to visit Iceland and asked for a guide that was local but could also communicate in French; She also taught French courses on the Icelandic State Television and had an impressive audience. From 1976 to 1980 she was a member of the Advisory Committee on Cultural Affairs in Nordic Countries. In 1996, she became the founding chair of the Council of Women World Leaders at the John F. Kennedy School of Government at Harvard University; two years later she was appointed president of the United Nations Educational Scientific and Cultural World Commission on the Ethics of Scientific knowledge and Technology. During the International Women's year in 1975 Icelandic women came to world attention when they organized a general strike to show the importance of women. 90% of Icelandic women participated in that strike. And the focus was on electing a woman as president. She put her name in and was narrowly elected with 33.6% of the vote; her nearest rival got 32.1%. Was she qualified? She became so popular and was re-elected three more times, until the longest serving Icelandic president until Olafur Ragnar Grimsson past her in 2012 with 5 terms. Although the presidency is largely a ceremonial position, she took an active role in hosting Ronald Reagan & Mikhail Gorbachev in 1986.

Melania Trump

(484)

Melania Knavs, (*or Knauss*), was born 26 April, 1970 in Slovenia Yugoslavia, her father Viktor Knavs managed a car and motorcycle dealership, her mother Amalija worked in children's clothing. She grew up in a modest apartment in a housing block in Sevnica. With assistance of the local priest Melania was secretly baptized as Catholic. After high school she attended the Secondary School of Design and Photography and studied architecture and design at the University of Ljubljana for a year then dropped out to begin commercial modeling; at that time she dropped the Slovene version of her last name "Knavs" changing it to the German version of "Knauss". Her parents had put her in modeling at age 5 and began doing commercial work at age 16, and at 18 signed on with an agency in Milan Italy. She did modeling for fashion houses in Paris and Milan and met Paolo Zampolli, who was a friend of Donald Trump on a European scouting trip and asked her to move to the US, even offered to represent her. In 1996 she moved to New York and several years later in 2010 launched her own line of Jewelry as well a skin care products. Back in 2001 Melania was dating Donald Trump and had been granted permanent US residency on her H-1B visa, (*given to people with extra-ordinary abilities*). Her path to citizenship was totally legal; she became engaged to Donald Trump in 2004. The media questioned her during Trump's campaign for the Reform Party; when asked by the New York Times: "What would your role be should he get the nomination, and become president?" She replied: "*I would be very traditional, like Betty Ford or Jackie Kennedy.*" They were married on January 22, 2005 in an Anglican service at the Episcopal Church of Bethesda-by-the-Sea in Palm Beach Florida, followed by a reception at the *Mar-a-Lago,* the Estate of Donald Trump. The marriage was her first and his third; it was attended by many celebrities such as Matt Lauer, Katie Couric, Regis Philbin, New York City Mayor Rudy Giuliani, Heidi Klum, Barbara Walters, Simon Cowell, Bill & Hillary Clinton, and many more; the ceremony, and the reception was widely covered by major media, including *Vogue-Cover* which featured her in her US$200,000 wedding gown made by John Galliano of the house of Christian Dior. In 2006 she gave birth to their son Barron; later that year Melania became a naturalized American citizen. For America she is the second naturalized woman, after Louisa Adams who was the first non-native English speaking person to become First Lady of John Quincy Adams, they had met in London; his parents did not support him marrying an English lady, but that did not stop him. Trump was elected to be the President of the United States and Melania became America's First Lady, a major accomplishment for a new arrival and a lady of great dignity.

John Winthrop

(485)

John Winthrop was born on 12 Jan. 1587 in Edwardstone Suffolk England, to Adam & Anne Winthrop. The family had been successful in the textile business and his father was a lawyer and prosperous landowner. *When I first read it I was jealous, but should I be?* In the late 1620's England's religious atmosphere began to look bleak for the Puritans & other groups of the English Reformation; why? King Charles-1 ascended to the throne in 1625, married Henrietta Maria (<u>Roman Catholic</u>), and opposed all teachings and practices of the Puritans, these were not just his opinions but he created an atmosphere of intolerance and then things got worse, in March 1629 the king dissolved Parliament beginning 11 years of rule without Parliament. Puritans began to see the handwriting on the wall began making plans to escape to the New World as a viable means for a better life. The first successful religious colonization occurred in 1620. When the departure time came for the next wave, Winthrop's wife was about to give birth so it was decided that she would follow with the next group. About 400 departed but 200 did not survive the small pox epidemic and on June 12, 1630 John Winthrop stood at the rail of <u>*Lady Arbella*</u> with the new arrivals of 200 entered the Salem harbor after 72 days at sea, at the end of a risky undertaking they finally had arrived; but was it what they expected? John Endicott, (the acting governor in the New World), informed him that of the preceding settlers more than 80 had died, and the rest had returned to England, of those remaining they were planning to do the same. As Winthrop surveyed the disheartening situation what should he do now? <u>He said</u>: *"Now the only way to provide posterity is to follow the counsel of Micah, to do justly, to love mercy, to walk humbly with our God. We shall labor and suffer together always having before our eyes our commission …..and keep the unity of the spirit in the bond of peace. The God of Israel is among us… ten of us shall be able to resist thousands of our enemies and we shall be as a city upon a hill."* <u>Rekindled in his vision,</u> John Winthrop went on to serve as the governor of Massachusetts till his death at age 61 in 1649, he was the key instrument in shaping Massachusetts into a Christian Commonwealth that went on to have a profound effect on the rest of the developing new nation. John Winthrop conquered his initial disappointment, because God gave him a vision of the future. This was his rationale: <u>He delivered Arbella,</u> <u>argued for the creation for a community covenanted with God</u> <u>formed a representative government.</u> *<u>Prov. 13:12 "Hope deferred makes the heart sick, but a longing fulfilled is a tree of life."</u>*

William Prescott

(486)

William Prescott was born 20 February, 1726 in Groton, Massachusetts. To Benjamin & Abigail Prescott; he was still quite young when he served in the Provincial militia as a lieutenant when the troops which were sent to remove the neutral-French from Nova Scotia in 1755. After his return he married miss Abigail Hale on April 13, 1758, it did not take long for him to get promoted to the office of captain and when the French & Indian war had widened he saw action at the Battle of Fort Beausejour. Being a superb warrior he was offered to join the British Army but turned it down. In the militia after he rose to the rank of Captain it did not take long for him to get promoted to colonel. On 19 April 1775 the alarm was raised that British troops were marching on Concord, reached Pepperell about 10 AM. Prescott hastened on with as many of his regiment he could collect to Concord and on to Cambridge but did not overtake the retreating British troops and arrived too late. When the American military commanders were alerted to British plans to capture undefended high ground at Dorchester Heights and Charlestown, Prescott was chosen to lead 1200 men and march onto the Charlestown peninsula, there erect defenses on Bunker Hill. The detachment started at Bunker Hill at 11PM and worked all night building trenches, Colonel

Prescott was a very tall man 6 ft 3 inches they knew they had to dig deep and lay the ground work on defending the area, building all the barricades they could muster. Prescott's was known for his signature order to the soldiers, "*Do not fire until you see the white of their eyes*." When it became known to the troops they knew that shooting the enemy at shorter range, were a brilliant concept as the targets were reached more accurately and lethally and so conserve their limited supplies of ammunition. At the heat of battle Prescott would take the lead and walk leisurely around cheering on his troops and encourage them. His clothing was repeatedly spattered with blood & brains of the killed and wounded. His coat had several holes pierced by bayonets indicating he was always in front of his troops. The men had been digging trenches all night were getting tired when the battle was hot, his encouragements were sorely needed. When the second Continental Congress established the Continental Army it sent George Washington to command of the forces besieging Boston. Colonel Prescott received command of the 7th Continental Regiment and they defended New York. Prescott did not have the advantages of an early education; he was a self-made man and most likely retired due to injuries. He left a legacy that is coveted by many who ever held leadership positions. Wars are different today but the principles of leadership are inside a man and generally not inherited. Prescott was a leader, he died at age 69 on Oct 13, 1795 in Mass.

Adam Smith

(487)

Adam Smith was born on 5 June 1723 in Fife Scotland, his father was a Scottish writer, Senior Solicitor, Prosecutor and served as Comptroller of the customs; his mother was Margaret Douglas. Two months before birth his father died, but mom pursued a scholarly education for him and he entered the Glasgow University at age 14 studied moral Philosophy under Francis Hutchison, and developed a passion for the philosophical concepts of reason, civilian liberties and free speech. Smith was a pioneer in the thinking of political economy and key figure during the Scottish Enlightenment; seen by some as The Father of Economics or the Father of Capitalism. He wrote two classic works: *The Theory of Moral Sentiments* (1759) and *The Wealth of Nations* (1776), (often considered the first modern work that treats economics as a comprehensive system and as an academic discipline). Smith refuses to explain the distribution of wealth and power in terms of God's will and instead appeals to natural, political social, economic and technological factors and the interactions between them. After graduating he delivered a successful series of public lectures at the University of Edinburgh, leading him to collaborate with David Hume during the Scottish Enlightenment. As a reaction to the common policy of protecting national markets and merchants

Smith laid the foundations of classical free market economic theory; the Wealth of Nations could be seen as a precursor to the modern academic discipline of economics. He developed the concept of division of labor, which in some ways was controversial. There seem to be two people that influenced him quite a bit: Francis Hutchison & David Hume (*The latter see our book #3 as 406 on page 10*). Smith rarely sat for portraits so almost all depictions of him were drawn from memory. Considerable scholarly debate has occurred about Smith's religious views; his father was known to have strong interest in Christianity and belonged to the moderate wing of the Church of Scotland. Some have suggested he was a deist based on the fact that his writings never explicitly invoke God as an explanation of the harmonies of the natural or the human world. According to Anglo-American economist Ronald Coase Smith does refer to the "<u>*Great Architect of the Universe*</u>". In 1759 Smith published *The Theory of Moral Sentiments*; in there he critically examines the moral thinking of his time. Former US Federal Reserve Chairman Alan Greenspan argues that Smith brought conceptual clarity to the seeming chaos of market transactions. Adam Smith died at age 67 on 17 July 1790 in Edinburgh Scotland, and has been celebrated by advocates of free market policies as the founder of free market economics. His book the Wealth of Nations was named in 2005 among the <u>Best Scottish books of all time</u>.

Pat Boone

(488)

Patrick Charles Eugene Boone was born 1 June, 1934 in Jacksonville Florida to Archie Altman Boone & Margaret Virginia. When Pat was two years old the family moved to Nashville Tennessee where he was raised. In Nov 1953 at age 19 he married Chicago born Tennessean Shirley, and stayed married till she died at age 84. Together they had 4 daughters Cherry, Lindy, Debby, & Laury. Shirley had founded a hunger relief Christian ministry. Pat began his career by performing in Nashville's Centennial Park and started recording in 1953. They grew up in the Church of Christ and in the 1960's the marriage nearly came to an end because of his preference for parties & use of alcohol. But Shirley came in contact with the Charismatic Movement and focused on her Christian faith; she influenced Pat and their daughters toward the same. At that time the family attended Inglewood Church. In the spring of 1964, Pat spoke at a "*Project Prayer*" rally, attended by 2500 in Los Angeles (including) several major stars of the entertainment world. The Boone's may not have been a perfect family but they came through the unprincipled Hollywood carnage and demonstrated a life of success by modeling an uncompromised Christian family in a dark world. We first encountered Pat Boone in 1960 when we were married in New Zealand and honeymooned in a small resort town. Due to a major newspaper article, we were recognized even though we had expected an incognito honeymoon, but after that media story our cover became local news and the town hosted us the entire two weeks closing with a free movie night in the Town Hall, *April Love* Starring Pat Boone & Shirley Jones. That time Hollywood produced some good material. Later in the early 1970's Pat hosted Bible Studies for celebrities such as Doris Day, Glenn Ford, Zsa Zsa Gabor, Priscilla Presley and many more. Pat had access to media and used much of his talent to bring glory to his Creator. Other people in Hollywood may have been Christian, but the Pat Boone family made attempts to live an open Christian life, even though his rival was Elvis Pressley, Pat recorded numerous songs and sold 45 million records worldwide; has 13 gold singles, 2 gold albums, a platinum album, and has recorded over 2,300 songs, more than any recording artist in recorded music history. He's starred in 15 movies, including 1957's Bernardine, and he has three stars on the Hollywood Walk of Fame. In 2003 Boone was inducted into the Gospel Music Hall of Fame, along with Amy Grant, and the Blind Boys of Alabama. Pat & Shirley Boone were high school sweethearts & married over 65 years. When Shirley died Pat said: She has changed her address and moved to a different mansion and I expect to join her in one day. Pat has left us a treasure of music legacy of Patriotic Marches, Anthems, & Hymns; he's made a difference.

Charles Hodge

(489)

Charles Hodge was born Dec. 27, 1797 the son of a Scotchman who had emigrated from Northern Ireland early in the 18th century. His father Hugh died from the yellow fever 7 months after he was born. His mother Mary took in boarders and put the boys through school. She provided the customary Presbyterian religious education using the Westminster Shorter Catechism; Charles grew up and went to Princeton Theological Seminary and became a Reformed Presbyterian Theologian and principal of Princeton Theological Seminary between 1851 & 1878. At Princeton the first president of the new seminary Archibald Alexander took special interest in Hodge assisting him in Greek and taking him along on itinerant preaching trips and became a leading exponent of the Calvinist Theological tradition in America during the 19th century; he argued strongly for the authority of the Bible as the Word of God. He had become a brilliant scholar. His ideas were adopted in the 20th century by Fundamentalists and Evangelicals. Hugh had graduated from Princeton College in 1773 & served as military surgeon in the Revolutionary War after which he practiced medicine in Philadelphia. He married Mary Blanchard in 1790; their lives suffered much tragedy, their first 3 sons died in the Yellow Fever Epidemic of 1795. Their first son to survive was born in 1796. Hugh Lenox, an authority on obstetrics remained especially close with Charles to be a friend through turbulent years. Hodge also befriended future Episcopalian Bishops John Johns and Charles McIlvaine & future Princeton College president John Mclean. In 1815, during a time of intense religious fervor among the students it was then that Hodge joined the local Presbyterian Church and entered the ministry at such a time. He had gone through rigorous studies where students were required to recite scripture in the original languages and to use the dogmatics written in Latin in the 17th century reformed scholastic Francis Terretin as a theological textbook. The professors also inculcated an intense piety in their students. Following graduation from Princeton Seminary in 1819 Hodge received additional instruction privately from Hebrew Scholar Joseph Bates in Philadelphia. He was licensed to preach by the Presbytery of Philadelphia in 1820. Then he studied another 2 years in Europe and traveled the continent to round of his education. Hodge wrote many biblical and theological works and continued publishing his writings till he died. In 1874 he published *What is Darwinism*? And concluded its atheism. Hodge was a Scholar, Educator, Churchman and Distinguished American theologian. He might have been one of the greatest scholars of all time. He died at age 80 on 19 June 1878, leaving a treasure trove of scholarly Works for Theological students and schools.

Irving Berlin

(490)

Irving Berlin was born *Israel Beilin* on 11 May, 1888 in a family of eight children in Siberia, Russian Empire, and came to the US on the <u>SS Rhynland</u> at age five with the family, arriving at Ellis Island in New York on Sept 14, 1893. His first memory takes him back to Siberia lying on a blanket by the side of the road watching his house burn to the ground. They were among thousands of Jewish families who immigrated to the US in the late 1800's and early 1900 escaping poverty discrimination, and heartless programs. As an adult he said he was unaware of being raised in abject poverty since he knew no other life. Berlin published his first song "*Marie from Sunny Italy*" in 1907 receiving 33 cents for the publishing rights, and had his first major hit "*Alexander's Ragtime Band*", in 1911. For much of his career he could not read sheet music and was able to play the piano only in key of F-sharp. At age 18 he got a job as a singing waiter at the Pelham Café in Chinatown; besides serving drinks he sang made up parodies of hit songs to the delight of customers. Long after the bar closed for the night, young Berlin would sit at the piano in the back improvising tunes. In 1908, at age 20 he took a new job at a saloon named Jimmy Kelly's in the Union Square neighborhood. There he was able to collaborate with other young songwriters. In 1911 he rose as a songwriter in Tin

Pan Alley and on Broadway, becoming an instant celebrity featuring in Oscar Hammerstein's vaudeville house where he introduced dozens of other songs, a *Time* profile of Berlin described "*Alexander's Ragtime band* as a march, not a rag; its savviest musicality comprised quotes from a bugle call and "*Swanee River*". From first and subsequent releases the song was near the top of the chart. Berlin learned fast what kind of songs appealed to audiences. One night he delivered some hits composed by his friend, George M. Cohan, (another kid who was getting known on Broadway). When Berlin ended with Cohan's "Yankee Doodle Boy" everybody in the joint applauded the feisty little fellow. It is not exactly known how many songs Berlin wrote but during his 60 year career it is estimated that there are at least 1,500, including the scores of more than 20 for Broadway shows and 15 original Hollywood films, with his songs nominated eight times for Academy Awards. Many of his songs have become all time American favorites such as *Alice in Wonderland, American Eagles, Happy Holidays, White Christmas, Blue Skies, God Bless America*, and many more. His songs have reached the top of the charts at least 25 times. Neither Russia nor Hitler wanted the innovative talents of the Jewish people but having been raised with Jewish kids in WW-II; it's my opinion that their loss is our gain. Irving Berlin died at age 101 in New York City on 22 Sept. 1989, but his legacy lives on.

Jerome

(491)

Jerome of Stridon was born 342-347 on the border of Strido Dalmatiae & Pannonia. He was a Christian Priest, confessor, theologian and historian and is commonly known as Saint Jerome. He is best known for his translation of the Bible in to Latin and his commentaries on the whole Bible. He was known for his teachings on Christian moral life especially to those living in cosmopolitan centers such as Rome. In many cases he focused his attention on the lives of women and identified how a woman devoted to Jesus should live her life. This focus stemmed from his close patron relationships with several prominent female ascetics who were members of affluent senatorial families. Due to his work he is recognized as a Doctor of the Church and by the Catholic, Lutheran, Anglican and Eastern Orthodox he is recognized as a Saint. When he first converted to Christianity he was afraid and seized with a life of ascetic penance and went for a time to the Syrian Desert finding time for studying & writing. He translated parts of the Hebrew Gospel into Greek, and updated the book of Psalms. He seemed to have been surrounded by women and is estimated that 40% of his epistles is addressed to the female sex. In his 30's he lived for 5 years on six ounces of barley bread. Due to the time he spent in Rome with wealthy families in the Roman upper-class he corresponded with these women about certain abstentions. He lived as an ascetic and is the second most voluminous writer after Augustine of Hippo (*354-430*); He also translated 14 Jewish religious books but saw a definite distinction between the 39 inspired books and the Apocrypha. His translation became known as the Vulgate. At the time of the Reformation, the pope called the Council of Trent to stem the tide of Protestantism. There in an attempt to differentiate the Roman Catholic Church from the Reformers the Council declared the Latin Vulgate, including the Apocrypha to be the authoritative Bible in matters of doctrine, while the Reformers recognized only the New Testaments and the original 39 books of the Old Testament. Even though Jerome had included the Apocrypha in the Vulgate as <u>uninspired</u> books; The Council of Trent declared them to be inspired, and is the difference between the Roman Catholic Bible and the Protestant Bible. The Catholic Bible contains 73 books and the Protestant Bible contains 66 books. Both do agree on 27 books in the New Testament but differ on the Old Testament. Protestants claim 66 books in the Old Testament and 27 in the New Testament. There are other differences such as RC do honor the pope as head of the church but the Protestants say Christ is; and pray to Him where RC pray also to holy man who passed away as well as Mary as the mother of God. See also #522 & 537 in this series. Jerome died at age 73-78) on 30 Sept. 420.

James Renwick

(492)

James Renwick was born 15 Feb. 1662 in Moniaive Scotland; his father Andrew was a weaver and his mother Elizabeth had born many children but all died in infancy. James had an affinity for God from an early age, by age 2 he was observed having serious prayer in the cradle. In 1675 his father died and James went on to the University of Edinburgh where he studied the Presbyterian religion of his forefathers. In 1681 he saw several Covenanters being martyred in Edinburgh, including Donald Cargill. In October 1681 he organized a secret meeting of this party. A correspondence was instituted between the societies of sympathizers in various parts of west Scotland. Sir Alexander Gordon of Earlston, who had been commissioned to Holland by the Societies in March 1682 made arrangements there, for Renwick to pursue his theological studies with a view to ordination. After the martyrdom of Cargill the United Societies were without a minister in Scotland they could acknowledge, but sent Renwick to Holland to get theological training from Dutch professors and orderly installments in the sacred office from Dutch presbyters and from the middle of 1681 to the end of 1683, they had neither preaching nor sacraments. Renwick spent a session at the University of Groningen and Leeuwarden. His ordination was performed by Sir Robert

Hamilton with Wilhelmus Brakel a Dutch divine. He objected to the Dutch liturgical forms and was allowed to substitute the Westminster Confession & Catechism. His ordination certificate is dated 9 April 1683. On 10 May he received commendatory letters from the Groningen classis and proceeded to Briel (Belgium), to embark on the return voyage. He abandoned the first ship on account of profane passengers and pressing him to drink to the king's health; he transferred to a vessel bound for Ireland. But now Roman Catholic James VII became king of Scotland in 1685, just at a time that Renwick was on his way back to Scotland and upon arrival he entered the ministry, but was soon proclaimed a rebel by the Scottish Privy Council. His position was misrepresented and sometimes he & his followers crept into churches by night and held their meetings. Efforts were made to apprehend him but after some early attempts he escaped. Renwick refused to join the insurrection of 1685 under Archibald Campbell, although he was sympathetic. His old friend Sir Alexander Gordon turned against him along with some others. 100 pounds reward was offered to anyone who would deliver Renwick dead or alive. His friends were faithful and they moved around the country even narrowly escaping a number of attempts, but eventually he was captured in 1688, tried, found guilty, and at only age 26 hanged on 17 Feb. 1688. It was the last execution, the king was exiled a year later and the persecution was over.

D, James Kennedy
(493)

Dennis James Kennedy was born 3 Nov. 1930 in Augusta Georgia US; his father was a glass salesman and the family was Methodist; they first moved to Chicago where he joined the Boy Scouts, later the family transferred to Florida where he grew up. He became a dance instructor at the Arthur Murray studio and met Anne Lewis there whom he later married. In 1953 he listened to a radio preacher presenting the Gospel which he had never heard that clear up to that point, decided to quit the dance lessons and pursue ministry, got a Divinity degree from Columbia Theological Seminary and a doctorate on Evangelism History to dispel the idea there is an inconsistency between Evangelism & education... Evangelism ministers need to be thoroughly educated and equipped to meet on equal terms with anyone. He later founded *Evangelism Explosion.* Kennedy was initially ordained in 1959 in the Presb. Church in America but left the denomination in 1978. Adhering to traditional Calvinist Theology his theological works include: *What if Jesus had never been born, Why I believe, Truths that Transform, Skeptics Answered*, and many more. He preached his first sermon at the Coral Ridge Presbyterian Church in Ft Lauderdale June 1959, beginning with 45 persons, grown to 1366 members by 1968. Evangelist Billy Graham spoke at the dedication of the new building in 1974, attended by 15,000 people; Kennedy expressed his entrepreneurial vision for outreach at the dedication stating: "*It is our prayer, that through this church, the Gospel of Jesus Christ might be radiated through television & radio, books & clinics, and by ways yet undreamed of into the entire world, that the command of Christ to go and proclaim the Gospel to every creature might be fulfilled in our generation.*" He developed *Evangelism Explosion* in the 1960s' which emphasizes the training of church laypeople to share their faith by home visitation and everyday encounters in the community, (*we initiated that in Hawaii*). He began the weekly Coral Ridge Hour, (*now Truths that Transform*) on National Television which at its peak had a weekly audience of 3 million viewers in 200 countries aired on more than 400 stations and four cable networks as well as broadcast to more than 150 countries and the Armed Forces Network. Many of his public messages focused on American History and the Faith of our Fathers of the United States. He celebrated Reagan's election but cautioned his congregation in a sermon titled *Can Reagan save America*? Warning people that it's not politics that saves America but only the Gospel of Christ. He strongly opposed Same Sex Marriage. In the late 70's he was a founding member of the Moral Majority. By the 1980s, his church membership had grown to almost 10,000. On September 5, 2007 D, James Kennedy at age 76 died in Fort Lauderdale.

Walter Williams

(494)

Walter Edward Williams was born 31 March, 1936 in Philadelphia Penn. US His mother raised him and his father played no role during his childhood years. The Family lived in the *Richard Allen Housing Project* till he was ten years old; Bill Cosby was one of his neighbors they had many of the same friends. After graduating from Benjamin Franklin High School he went to California to live with his father and attended Los Angeles City College for one semester, but moved back to Philadelphia working as a cab driver for Yellow Cab Company and in 1959 he went in the US Army. While stationed in the South he waged a one man battle against *Jim Crow* from inside the army. He challenged the racial order with provocative statements to his fellow soldiers that did not go to well because an officer filed court martial proceedings against him. Williams argued his own case and was found <u>not guilty</u>. He filed a countercharge against the officer, but was transferred to Korea. Upon arriving there he marked Caucasian for race; when challenged he said if I put Black I would end up getting crappy jobs. He wrote a letter to President John Kennedy denouncing the pervasive racism in the American military and wrote: "*Should Negroes be relieved of their service obligation or continue defending and dying for empty promises of freedo0m & equality? Or should we*

demand human rights as our Founding Fathers did at the risk of being called extremists?" He received a reply from the Deputy Assistant Secretary of Defense, Alfred Fitt. After his military service he went to school and earned a bachelors degree in Economics in 1965 from California State College, Los Angeles. He earned both his Masters and PhD in economics from UCLA, and worked as an instructor in economics at Los Angeles. Speaking of his early college days he really wanted to be left alone. At UCLA he came in contact with economist such as James Buchanan and others who challenged his assumptions. Although Williams was a strong proponent of free market economics and opposed socialist systems of government intervention. In his nearly 50 years career he wrote hundreds of research articles, book reviews, and commentaries for scholarly journals, including *American Economic Review*, *Policy Review*, *Newsweek*, *The Wall Street Journal* and many more. He wrote more than ten books and hosted documentaries on National Television. He was opposed to the Federal Reserve System arguing that central banks are dangerous. He authored a weekly column and was often referred to as one of the country's leading libertarian voices. He died at age 84 on 1 December 2020 in Fairfax VA.

James Guthrie

(495)

James Guthrie was born about 1612 in Scotland, went to the University, and Graduated with an M.A. from St Andrews; he subsequently became a Regent in St Leonard's college. He was sent with a few others to go to Charles-1 with a letter from the assembly in 1646, and preached before Parliament on 10 January, 1649. After that became commissioner to the University in Edinburgh he took an active part in the business of the Church and along with a small group got General John Middleton excommunicated, (*Kincardinshire mercenary from Scotland during the 30 year war of the Parliamentarians & the Covenanters*), although he appealed to the king. He and his colleague were required by His Majesty and the Committee of Estates to repair the <u>Perth,</u> (*not mean a city in Western Australia, but here it refers to irritating),* to answer for preaching against Public Resolutions agreed by the Church and State, <u>but they refused</u>. He was deposed by the Assembly for having joined the Protest. He & others holding similar views formed a separate church under the protection of Cromwell. During a congratulatory address in Edinburgh he was seized and imprisoned in the Castle on 23 August 1660; then on 25 May, 1661 he was tried before the well named <u>*drunken Parliament*</u>, found guilty of treason, sentenced to death and hanged on 1 June 1661, his estate was confiscated. Before the hanging he addressed the crowd he said: "...*My blood will contribute more for the propagation of these things than my life in liberty would do; Jesus Christ is my life and my Righteousness; now Lord let thy servant depart in piece.* The sentence was rescinded by Parliament and his scull, after being a public spectacle for about 28 years was removed by Alexander Hamilton. From his determined support of Presbyterian Principle, Guthrie was considered their leader. The origin of the dispute goes back to the year 1647, about a secret treaty between him and representatives from Scotland which he accepted, and was known as the *Engagement*, approved by the Scottish Parliament but was condemned by the Commission of the Assembly of the Church of Scotland, it instructed every minister to preach against it. It was a bold step of Guthrie to oppose King Charles-1. Those who signed the Covenant were committed to the Reformed Faith and for Reformers it was a dangerous time. Guthrie took a chance to meet the town hangman and said I know I shall die for what I have done but I can not die for a better cause. He served through the first and second English Civil War. Guthrie led a group of 12 Scotsmen to petition the king, but the king threw all of them in prison. He was willing to die for what he believed, and was about 49 when he died as one of the first martyrs, on 1 June 1661, (*James Renwick was the last in 1688*).

Emma Lazarus

(496)

Emma Lazarus was born 22 July, 1849 in New York City and was the fourth of seven children of Moses Lazarus, a wealthy Jewish merchant and sugar refiner and Esther Nathan. One of her grandfathers on the Lazarus side was from Germany, the rest of the Lazarus Nathan ancestors were from Portugal. She was privately educated by tutors and from an early age Emma studied American and British literature as well as several languages including Italian German, & French. She was still young when attracted to poetry, writing her first lines at age 11. Between her ages 14 to 17 the stimulation came to her through actions all around her during the years of the American Civil War. In the next decade she wrote "Phantasies" and "Epochs" her poems appeared chiefly in *Lippincott's monthly Magazine* and *Scribner's Monthly*. By now she had won recognition abroad. Her first prose production, *Alida; An Episode of Goethe's Life, a romance treating of the Friederike Brion incident* was published in (1874) followed by *The Spagnoletto* (1876) Tragedy, Poems and Ballads of Heinrich Heine (New York, 1881), followed, and was prefixed by a biographical sketch of Heine; Lazarus rendering of some of Heine's verse are considered among the best in English. In that same year she became friends with Rose Hawthorne Lathrop. In April 1882, Lazarus published in *The Century Magazine* the article "*Was the Earl of Beaconsfield a Representative Jew?*" The period of Lazarus life, during which her subjects were drawn from classic and romantic sources. The literary fruits of identification with her religion were poems like "*The Crowing of the Red Cock*," "*The Banner of the Jew*", "*The Choice*", "*The New Ezekiel*" "*The Dance with Death*" (1887). She returned to New York seriously ill after her second trip to Europe. Emma Lazarus is mostly remembered for her writing *The New Colossus* (1883) of which a few lines was placed on a plaque of the Statue of Liberty pedestal, reminding us of unfettered and unrestricted immigration. The key lines of Emma Lazarus are: "*Give me your tired, your poor, your huddled masses yearning to breathe free…I lift my lamp beside the golden door…*" She donated the poem to raise money for the construction of the pedestal of the Statue of Liberty donated by France to America in 1885; upon completion the statue was dedicated on 28 October 1886. President Grover Cleveland presided over the event. Emma Lazarus most likely suffered from Hodgkin's lymphoma. She never married and died at age 38 on 19 Nov.1887 in NY City leaving a legacy of these meaningful words. We are immigrants and visited the Statue of Liberty in 1964 it deeply moved us when the words and the author were explained. Emma is no longer here but the statue goes on speaking.

Don Knotts

(497)

Jesse Donald Knotts was born 21 July, 1924 in Morgantown, West Virginia US. He was the youngest of four sons of William Jesse Knotts and Elsie Luzetta Moore; his father had schizophrenia and alcohol problems and died of pneumonia when Don was 13, Elsie was 40 at his birth; as a young widow she ran a boardinghouse while raising 4 boys alone. Before Don entered high school he began performing as a ventriloquist and comedian at various church and school functions. After high school, he traveled to New York City trying to make his way as a comedian but his career failed to take off forcing him to return to West Virginia. After his freshman year, he joined the US Army and spent most of his service entertaining troops. He toured the Western Pacific Islands as a comedian in a G.I. variety show called "*Stars & Gripes*". His ventriloquist act included a dummy named Danny, which he grew to hate and eventually threw him overboard. He served in the army from 21 June 1943, to 6 January 1946, most of that time was in World War-II, in *the 6817th Special Services Battalion*, and was discharged at the rank of Technician Grade 5 (equivalent to a corporal). He was awarded several medals, even four bronze service stars. After being demobilized Don returned to West Virginia University and graduated in 1948. He married Kay Metz and moved back to NY where he tried show business, beginning with stand-up comedies at clubs. His break came when he got a role in a TV soap opera *Search for Tomorrow*. In 1956 he got success on the Steve Allen's variety show most notably in Allen's mock "*Man on the Street*" interviews, always playing an extremely nervous man and remained in there through the 1960 season. From 1955 to 1957 he appeared on the Broadway stage version of *No Time for Sergeants* where he played two roles. In 1958 he made his movie debut with Andy Griffith; In 1960 Andy Griffith got his own sitcom, and Don Knotts took the role of Barney Fife, the Deputy Sheriff, earning him five Emmy Awards for Best Supporting Actor in TV Comedy. In there he has been described as: Romantic, nearly always wrong, he dreamed of the day he could use the one bullet Andy had issued to him; he always fired his pistol accidentally while still in the holster, or in the ceiling of the courthouse. He kept one shiny bullet in his shirt pocket. He suffered from hypochondria and macular degeneration and his fellow actors described his as a very quiet man, very sweet. He was married three times and had a son and a daughter. He entertained almost every American and was one of the most beloved persons in show business. He died at age 81 on 24 February, 2006, I miss him.

James O'Keefe

(498)

James Edward O'Keefe was born 28 June 1984 in Bergen County, New Jersey US. He got his B.A in philosophy at Rutgers University; after that he gained national attention for his undercover video recordings. For a while he worked with the Leadership Institute in Virginia under media specialist Ben Wetmore, whom O'Keefe calls his mentor. The institute sent him to colleges to train students how to start conservative independent student newspapers; he was very effective doing that, and released many secretly recorded videos receiving much media coverage of workers at <u>Association of Community Organizations for Reform Now</u>, (ACORN). In 2010 he changed his organization to Project Veritas, whose stated mission is to investigate and expose corruption, dishonesty, self-dealing, waste, fraud, and other misconduct in both public and private institutions in order to achieve a more ethical and transparent society. Much of the funding comes from donations in the private sector, we are among his supporters. Even prominent donors such as Trump donated much to the organization. After videos were released in the fall of 2009, the US Congress quickly voted to freeze federal funding to ACORN, especially when the negative publicity got much public attention; The Census Bureau and the IRS terminated their contract relationship.

By December 2009, an external investigation of ACORN was published which cleared the organization of <u>any</u> illegality. On 1 March, 2010 Brooklyn District Attorney Charles J. Hynes found there was no criminal wrongdoing by the ACORN staff in New York. The California Attorney General's office granted O'Keefe limited immunity from prosecution in exchange for providing the full unedited videotapes related to ACORN offices in California. In 2016 he noticed vans were busing people around the polls in Philadelphia after which he released a series of videos titled "*Rigging the lection;*" The videos led to the arrest of three people who pleaded guilty, in that same year O'Keefe released another series that people were at the front lines at the rallies to ask the right questions; a common practice known as "*bird dogging*". Finally it was O'Keefe who filed a complaint with the Federal Election Commission (FEC) against Hillary Clinton and the DNC and 3 left leaning super PAC's, perhaps one of the greatest and most powerful criminal enterprises in the entire country. It seems that this time James O'Keefe may have stepped in the lion's den, or the snake pit. May God protect him, his motives are pure. O'Keefe made a difference big time he belongs here, America needs him.

Oliver North

(499)

Oliver Laurence North was born 7 October 1943 in San Antonio Texas US. The son of Oliver Clay North a US Army Major, and Ann Theresa Clancy, together they had four children. He graduated from Ockawimick Central High School in 1961, after that went to the State University in Brockport NY for 2 years. Then got an appointment to the US Naval Academy in 1963, and received his commission as second lieutenant. He was involved in a serious auto accident giving him _back & leg_ injuries, but a classmate was killed. One of his classmates was Jim Webb who later became the Secretary of the Navy. North served as a platoon commander during the Vietnam War, his unit took heavy machine gun fire and rocket propelled grenades; and throughout the battle North displayed courage, dynamic leadership, and unwavering devotion to duty in the face of grave personal danger, he was awarded the Silver Star, Bronze Star for Combat and two Purple Heart medals. In 1970 North returned to South Vietnam to testify as a character witness at the trial of Lance Corporal Randall Herrod, who along with four others had been charged with the murder of 16 Vietnamese civilians in the village of Son Thang, North claims that Herrod had saved his life. After the trial, the accused was acquitted. In 1981 Ollie was assigned to the National Security Council in

Washington DC where he served as a lobbyist from 1981 to 1983; while there he was promoted to Lieutenant Colonel and managed a number of missions; one of them he was assigned to hunt for those responsible for the 1983 Berut barracks bombing that killed 299 military personnel. While at the Security Council North helped plan the US Invasion of Grenada and the 1986 bombing of Libya. Then came the Iran Contra Affair, a political issue where he was accused of selling weapons to the enemy. North was convicted on 16 felony counts. Judge Gerhard Gesell sentenced him, to a three-year suspended prison term, two year's probation, $150,000 in fines, and 1,200 hours of community service. (*He performed some of his community service within Potomac Gardens, a public housing project in southeast Washington DC*). On appeal all charges were reversed and North was cleared of all wrongdoing. Not being familiar with all the details, perhaps someone did not agree with the wars North had been fighting, had a gripe with a decorated war hero and was perhaps in disagreement with the wars that North was involved with. It is common knowledge that the Viet Nam war was very unpopular. (For full disclosure, I am an ex-Marine during the Korean War); in my opinion Oliver North is a person who served his country honorably, earned many decorations and medals and was promoted to lieutenant Colonel. He has written many books and certainly belongs here among all those who made a difference.

Israel Kamakawiwo'ole

(500)

Israel Ka'aqno'i Kamakawiwo'ole was born 20 May 1959 in Honolulu Haw. His parents both worked at a popular Waikiki nightclub, mother as manager and father as bouncer who in the daytime drove a sanitation truck at the US Navy shipyard at Pearl Harbor. (Israel known as Brother IZ), began playing music at age 11 with his older brother Henry and cousin Allen. He was exposed to Hawaiian entertainers such as Keola Beamer, Don Ho, and many others. Hawaiian musician Del Beazley spoke of the first time he heard IZ perform at a graduation party, <u>the whole room fell silent on hearing him sing</u>. In his early teens he studied at Upward Bound (UB) of the University of Hawaii in Hilo, but then his family moved to Makaha; there he met several Hawaiian entertainers and formed *The Makaha sons of Ni'ihau*. The band gained in popularity and toured Hawaii as well as the mainland USA releasing fifteen successful albums and became one of the most popular contemporary break-out groups in Hawaii. He married Marlene, who was his childhood sweetheart; they had one daughter Ceslie-Ann Kamakawiwo'ole. In 1990 IZ released his first solo album *Facing Future*, it was an award winning contemporary album featuring his most popular songs: "<u>Somewhere over the rainbow</u>/ *What a wonderful world* / *White sandy beach* / *Maui Hawaiian Sup'pa Man* / and *Kaulana*

Kawaihae. It became Hawaii's first certified platinum selling more than a million CD's. We met IZ near the International Market Place may be two or three times in Waikiki while sitting on the sidewalk singing and selling his CD's to the tourists to whoever would stop and listen. We chatted a little between songs, he was very quiet spoken. We did not visit Waikiki often but mostly went when we had house-guests who wanted to go shopping or see Waikiki. There are always a lot of activities perhaps the closest semblance is Los Vegas with one difference: Vegas is all money oriented, where Hawaii is much more family oriented. IZ was also known for promoting Hawaiian rights and Hawaiian Independence; through his lyrics and his life he promoted the message of King Kamehameha III: <u>Ua Mau ke Ea o ka 'Aina I ka Pono</u>: "<u>*The life of the land is perpetuated in righteousness.*</u>" Waikiki attracts tourists from all over the world but it's not a 24 hour bonanza like Los Vegas. IZ had chronicle medical problems, he was 6 ft 2 and 750 lbs; he died from respiratory failure on 26 June 1997 at the Queen's Medical Center, in Honolulu, he was age 38 leaving a legacy of 50 great voice series. On 10 July 1997 his Koa wood casket lay at the State Capital, (the third non-government person to be so honored). 10,000 people attended his funeral, more drove by honking their horns. He made difference and belongs here.

Emma Veary

(501)

Emma Maynon Kaipuala Veary was born about 1930 in the territory of Hawaii and was a child prodigy, singing in church before she was old enough to go to school. As a child her role models were sopranos Jeanette MacDonald and Deanna Durbin. Her parents, both of Hawaiian ancestry encouraged her to pursue singing as a career but did not have the financial resources to provide her with musical training. She was put on a career path by teacher Irmgard (Gardie) Thompson leading to her singing on the radio and receiving favorable recognition, at age 10, she was profiled in the Honolulu Advertiser, which resulted in a music scholarship at Punahou School. She was about 10 years old when the Pacific war hit Hawaii with the bombing of 7 December, 1941. Even though Emma was only 10 or 11 years of age she became a USO performer while enrolled at Kamehameha School for girls, she joined with other singers such as John Kameaaloha Almeida to entertain the troops that were stationed at various military installations in the islands here in Hawaii. As a teenager she was sent to New York City to be trained at Carnegie Hall as a lyric Coloratura Soprano; while there she was exposed to the Broadway theatre productions of that era, and aspired to expand her repertoire to be inclusive of multiple forms of vocal expressions. Upon her return to

Honolulu she appeared one evening a week on radio station KGMB with Andy Cummings; she enrolled in Roosevelt High School, graduating in 1949, subsequently enrolling in the University as music major. In 1951 she married US Navy aviator Robert Moss and moved with him to California; there she raised 2 daughters, performed in stage productions, occasionally returning to Hawaii. In 1963 Emma divorced Moss and moved to New York to resume her career in musicals. In 1960 she returned to Hawaii and married local radio personality J. Akuhead Pupule, and become a staple in local stage productions at Waikiki hotel showrooms. She came to our office I was introduced to her by one of her daughters who was our client, we met her twice and she also became our client. At that time she was associated with the Halekulani Hotel in the Coral Terrace near the beach she invited me to be her guest one evening, but I never went. An article in the Honolulu Advertiser referred to Emma as a diamond in the proper setting. In her retirement she settled in Maui where the Emma Veary Music Scholarship was established for aspiring young musicians. In 2006 Emma Veary was inducted in the Hawaiian Music Hall of Fame. It was a great honor to meet Emma even though only briefly she is a special lady.

Kirsten Flagstad

(502)

Kirsten Malfrid Flagstad was born 12 July 1895 in Hamar Norway in her grandparent's home, (*now the Kirsten Flagstad Museum*). She never lived in Hamar but always considered it her hometown. She was mostly raised in Oslo within a musical family. Her father Michael was a conductor and her mother Maja was a pianist. Their other children were also musicians, such as pianist, singer, or conductor. Kirsten received her early musical training in Oslo making her stage debut at the National Theatre in 1913. She may have been one of the few sopranos who mastered Coloratura. In 1919 she married her first husband Sigurd Hall and a year later gave birth to her only daughter, Else Marie Hall. Later that year Kirsten signed up with the newly created *Opera Comique* in Oslo under the direction of Alexander Varnay (who was also the father of the most famous soprano Astrid Varnay). Kirsten sang at the Stora Theater of Gothenburg, Sweden between 1928 and 1934. In 1930 she married her second husband, Norwegian Industrialist Henry Johansen who helped her expanding her career. In 1932 she made her debut in *Rodelinda* by Handel. After singing operatic roles such as *Marguerite* in Faust for over a decade, she took on a heavier role in *Tosca* and *Aida*. It helped her unleash some dramatic abilities. In 1932, she took on the role of Isolde in Richard Wagner's Tristan and felt that she found her true voice. Kirsten was noticed in the summer of 1934 by Otto Hermann Kahn, chairman of the board of the Metropolitan Opera, she auditioned for Arthur Bodaqnzky who immediately engaged her. Her debut on 2 Feb. 1935 created a sensation even though Kirsten was unknown in the United States at that time, the performance was broadcast nationwide; the intermission host breathlessly announced that a new star had just been born. She became a pupil of the vocal coach Herman Weigert who prepared her for many roles. In 1952 her health was beginning to deteriorate and was in and out of hospitals, even joked with an interviewer in 1958 that Oslo hospital is my home away from home. She began to spend more time mentoring young singers in her native country, including Eva Gustavson. Some called her "the voice of the century." Desmond Shawe-Taylor said she ranks among the greatest singers of the 20th century; no one in living memory surpassed her in sheer beauty and consistency of line and tone. In her last years she gave benefit concerts throughout Norway. She was diagnosed with bone marrow cancer in 1960 and died of the disease on 7 December 1962. At her request she was buried in an unmarked grave in Vestre Gravlund Cemetary in the Frogner borough of Oslo. Her portrait appeared on the *Norwegian 100 kroner bill* and on the *tail section of Norwegian Air Shuttle planes*. Her Repertoire would fill several pages here.

Kristan Hawkins

(503)

Kristy Hawkins was born 28 August, 1980 in Longview Texas, after High School, she earned a Bachelor of Science in Chemical Engineering from Texas A&M University in 2002, graduating *summa cum laude with Honors*. She earned a Master of Science in Chemical Engineering at the California Institute of Technology (Caltech) in 2005 and graduated from there in 2008 with a Ph.D. In 1999 she worked as an intern for the Eastman Chemical Company Solutia Inc. From November 2008 to August 8, 2013, she was employed as a scientist. In 2013 worked as director of yeast engineering for the company Lygos. She left there and co-founded a chemical engineering company called Antheia. She described herself as having been heavy in elementary school, but eventually worked that out with exercise and other activities. She grew up and became a Christian, wife, mother, and anti-abortion grassroots activist, author, and speaker, and in 2006, she launched *Students for Life of America*. Kristan visits various college and high school campuses hoping to abolish abortion by transforming the culture. Recruit, train, and mobilize the younger generation which are a direct target of today's abortion industry. While in college she served at the Republican National Committee and was a presidential appointee in the George W. Bush administration at the Department of Health & Human

Services. Kristan was recruited to lead *Students for Life* in 2006, since then she has taken a small group of few dozen students pro-life groups scattered around the nation and has multiplied that number to over 1,200 organized Students for Life chapters helped in organizing that in all 50 states. She also served on Donald Trump's Pro-Life Advisory Council and is the author of *Courageous Students Abolishing Abortion in this Lifetime.* She's been interviewed on Fox News, CNN, MSNBC, the Today show, CBS, ABC & HBO and received the title: "One of the 4 worst anti-abortion misinformers" by Media Matters. She's proud of that title and keeps using it while speaking across the country reaching young people with her message. All of that while being married to her high-school sweetheart and raising their four children. In her spare time, she has been raising awareness for *Cystic Fibrosis*, a disease two of her children suffer from. Kristan hosts a weekly pod cast "*Explicitly Pro Life*" & is one of the most effective communicators for unborn children, having trained over 100,000 young people to spread the pro-life massage. In the Pro-Life arena I have debated the issue several times, (*seemingly centuries ago*) and after watching Kristy in a hostile classroom setting, I confess she is far superior then I ever was.

Danny Kaleikini

(504)

Danny Kaniela Kaleikini was born 10 October 1937 in Honolulu as one of eight children; he was of native Hawaiian, Chinese, Korean, Irish, and Italian descent. His father was in the Hawaii National Guard and worked as a refuse worker for the city. His mother Margie was a cocktail waitress at the Hilton Hawaiian Village Hotel. He learned the Hawaiian language from his mother and grandfather, at age five he sold newspapers as well as shined shoes in Chinatown and with his brother and friends he learned to sing and perform. In elementary school he played in the bell choir, at Kawananakoa Intermediate School and played the trumpet & the drums and was elected student body president. Later in Roosevelt High School he sang in the choir and performed in a 16-piece orchestra; he went to the University on a music scholarship. During his freshman year he worked part time at the Waikiki Sands. In 1967 he landed his show at the Luxury Kahala Hilton Hotel, (the first successful show outside Waikiki). Over time it became a *"must see"* show attended by US Presidents, foreign dignitaries and Hollywood celebrities. He did that for 28 years twice nightly. A review in 1971 called it a family show with friendly and clean jokes that would not make it in Waikiki. He opened the show with multi lingual greeting, and spoke Japanese to the tourists from Japan. He also played the rare Hawaiian nose flute, unique to Polynesians here in Hawaii and in the Pacific basin. In 1994 the Kahala Hilton hotel was sold to a foreign entity and after 20 years doing over 10,000 two-hour shows every night he retired. It had earned Danny a place in the Guinness book of world records. The hotel changed the front circle street to Danny Kaleikini Square, and. He often visited Japan and learned the language, was asked by Governor John Burns to attend Expo '70, the world's fare held in Osaka and coach the Hawaii performers. After that in 1973 Kaleikini was invited to the second annual Tokyo Music Festival to compete with singers from around the world; Danny was placed in the Music Hall of Fame on 2016 he was one of these entertainers' people immediately begun to love; he started every show with a hearty melodic Aloha, he was the real Aloha. Born and raised on homestead land he had a humble beginning and never lost that modesty, and said I learned all my songs from my father & grandfather. He was married to Jacqueline Wong and together they had 2 children both of whom performed with their father since age two; (one died of Pneumonia at age 29). Danny Kaleikini one of the finest Aloha Ambassadors Hawaii ever had, died at age 85 on 6 January 2023 in Honolulu.

Alina

(505)

Alina was born in Kiev. (We could not reach her to check if she is safe, therefore have changed the name to protect her identity, all other facts are hers). I was born into a large Ukrainian family and grew up in the former USSR where we were regularly persecuted; our childhood was good, filled with parental love, as children we looked after each other, but our books, music, and songs were tainted by communism. Mom saw to it we had a meal together and dad was a passionate evangelist at the local Baptist Church and made sure that we learned all the Bible stories. Dad was a pastor and planted new churches, encouraged fellow believers to remain firm in their faith. Our family was always in the communist radar. One time dad did not come home, we did not know where he was. Mom took us to the KGB office and demanded answers about where dad is, only _then_ he was taken out of his cell where he was held for his Christian belief. Often our family was awakened by a long doorbell ring all ours of the night. Once inside they searched our apartment for Christian literature, hymnals & Bibles; if found any, it was confiscated furniture was toppled, and our parents were criminals. Our neatly folded clothes and school books on the shelves were thrown everywhere. School was the same. I was ostracized by students and teachers. I know I was an outstanding student, in second grade it was an honor to be a "*first-aid-agent*", but was told I was not eligible because you are not a <u>Soviet led Octobrist</u>, If I joined I would have to abandon my family, and believe that Lenin was the greatest leader who ever lived; (*a little similar to Hitler youth in WW-II*). The school teachers and fellow students became very creative how to persecute me, such as lowering my grades. As a senior I knew I would get A on the algebra test, but got a barely passing grade; I went to the teacher who said my real grade was A+ but you know very well why your grade was a C. The family moved to the United States in an effort to get away from these pressures; in the 1980's in the US I met (YAF) Young America Foundation these young people inspired us to think for ourselves to engage in conversation and draw our own conclusions rather than follow the ideological tyranny of the Soviet Union. It's hard not to notice the recent attacks against freedom here on which this great country was founded. Ukrainians have a rich heritage dating back to the 12th century and understand that socialism is foolishness and we find it hard to imagine some here embrace it without experiencing it. Imagine being unable to get an education or not able to practice your religion or can not express your opinion, or being waitlisted to buy a car, a washer, or unable to buy a home due to your belief, may be its already too late here.

Nana Voitenko

(506)

Nana Voitenko was born and raised in Baku the capital of Azerbaijan one of the largest cities on the Caspian Sea in the Caucasus region, and is situated 92 ft (or 28 meters below sea level, making it the lowest national capital as well as the largest city in the world located below sea level. Baku is a major scientific, cultural and industrial center and is renowned for its harsh winds and nicknamed the City of Winds. When the war, *(the Armenian/Azerbaijani conflict 2021-2022)*, began her entire family migrated and dispersed around the world and had no home to return to. Nana graduated from the Moscow Institute of Physics and Technology, got married, and moved to Kyiv when it was still part of the USSR. She faced, and overcame, many challenges, that makes her story inspiring, extraordinary and courageous, she did not have a wide range of job opportunities at that time during the early 1990's there was already an active brain-drain in her field. A Moscow scientist would not be allowed to travel abroad, and her goal was to see the world; at that time Ukraine was still part of Russia, although the coming collapse became obvious and was being felt. Her master's degree was devoted to the study of calcium signaling in sensory neurons such studies in Moscow proved to be very useful, she met Platon Kostyuk, famous neurophysiologist chair of Biophysics at the Kyiv Branch of the MIPT, he was also the director of the Bogomoletz Institute of Physiology and the head of the Department of General Physiology of the Nervous System making her decision to abandon physics for neuroscience research, which turned out one of the best decisions she ever made. She began her PhD thesis devoted to the study of molecular mechanisms of calcium signaling in cerebellar neurons; and with that could begin to better understand the aging process in programmed pathology. The field of Neuroscience will be beneficial to Ukraine and reduce the brain drain of that nation allowing lab members to be paid a decent wage and should help Ukraine survive the war. After the collapse of the Soviet Union, former Soviet and now Ukrainian scientists were given the possibility to move freely around the world, go to conferences, workshops and able to share knowledge, it is invigorating when world scientists can share each other's discovery. By that time her colleagues had left to work in different laboratories in the UK, Germany, Canada and the US. In 1999, she received an independent grant from the Juvenile Diabetes Research Foundation, allowing her to begin her own laboratory, with early career scientists students and graduate students and was able to offer decent salaries to employees and purchase some modern equipment. She was a survivor and made a difference.

Al Harrington

(507)

Tausau Ta'a was born December 12, 1935 in Pago Pago, American Samoa. He was raised by his grandmother mostly in the village of Mapusaga in Pago Pago until he was three. His mother Lela Suapaia sent for him to join her while she was working as a nurse in Honolulu Hawaii. She later married Roy Milbur Harrington a native of Iron Mountain, Michigan who came to Honolulu with the US Army. It was not till his sophomore year in high school that he took his stepfather's last name. Al did well at theater and American football while he was in Punahou School, and was a member of the class of 1954. He participated in several productions at the school and at the same time wowed people on the football field. He led his team to the league championships at Honolulu Stadium and was the first high school football All-American to come out of Hawaii. Before transferring to Stanford University, he attended Menlo College, a private business school in Atherton Californian 1954 -1955. Then went on to play for Stanford and graduated in 1958 with a B.A. in History; at that time the Baltimore Colts were interested in him, but after exploring that, he decided to return to Honolulu, and worked as a Polynesian dancer, his most interesting background led to an appearance on the game show *To Tell The Truth*. Living back in Honolulu he worked as a history teacher at Punahou and as a professor at the University of Hawaii. In the evenings he performed as an entertainer in Waikiki earning the well-known moniker of "The South Pacific Man." His popularity in the 1970s and 1980s made him a household name in Hawaii. He had a long running dance revue show, including the Tahitian fire dance at the Hilton Hawaiian Village in Waikiki. It was there that he came by my office with some tickets and even though we rarely went to shows we did go and saw Al outside who led us to a VIP seating and it was special. At half time he announced that the show had a 20-minute break so he could go and talk to my friend Terry Bosgra who is here tonight. I thought that was very special and certainly received VIP treatment. Al Harrington helped define the entertainment industry in Honolulu known to tourists and dignitaries alike from around the world he was the type that brought together _old_ & _new_ Hawaii. He was also a cast member of Hawaii five-O TV series, along with Sharon Farrell and Dennis Chun and many others. He was a devout member of the Mormon Church and had a lead in the LDS film _The Testament_. Al Harrington died at age 85 in Honolulu, on 21 September, 2021 after suffering a massive stroke. He was my client and my friend and sometimes came by my office to chat a little; I miss him, he left behind a beautiful family.

Yeonmi Park

(508)

Yeonmi Park was born 4 October 1993 in Hyesan, Ryanggang Province, North Korea. Her father, Park Jin-Sik was a civil servant who worked at the Hyesan town hall as a member of the ruling <u>Workers' Party of Korea</u>, and her mother, Keum-Sook was a nurse for the Korean People's Army. Her father tried to supplement his meager income by smuggling clothes, rice, & Chinese cigarettes. He was caught, after a show trial and trumped-up charges he was sentenced to hard labor for illegally trading salt, sugar and other spices. In prison he endured malnutrition and inhumane treatment the family promised the warden a large bribe and he was released and united with his family. She changed her views of the ruling Kim-Regime after watching an illegal DVD of the movie *Titanic*, which caused her to realize the oppressive nature of her government, it taught her the true meaning of freedom & love. Her fathers' expulsion from the Workers' Party forced his children out of school and their living standard compelled them to move. Then her mother was arrested for illegally changing their residence. Her father suggested they escape to China, and did so, but he was too sick to cross the frozen river he had inoperable colon cancer. Christian missionaries helped them cross the border, although her sister Eunmi fell in the hands of human traffickers and was never heard from again. Her father did not make it. In China they assumed that her sister Eunmi had died. Park & her mother found a Christian shelter and traveled through the Gobi Desert to Mongolia, at the border the guards threatened to deport them back to North Korea, but Yeonmi & her mother decided to kill themselves rather than going back, and as they were hugging goodbye to each other; their actions persuaded the guards. They only had 2nd grade education and were sold to traffickers of human slavery, and ended up in Ireland where she gave a speech that got world attention, reaching 50 million people; due to imperfect memory, and limited linguistic skills her story had some inconsistencies. She went to Columbia University, School of General Studies majoring in economics. Her memoir _A North Korean Girl's journey to Freedom_ was published in 2015. She now runs the You Tube channel _Voice of North Korea by Yeonmi Park_, and on that covers Politics, North Korea News, and Culture. In 2022 she announced that her 2nd book _A North Korean Defector's search for freedom_ will be released in February 2023. Since escaping, Park has written and spoken publicly about her life in North Korea and has volunteered for an activist program such as a Freedom Factory Corporation, something like _a Free Market Think Tank._ This young lady is brilliant; North Korea's brain drain is a plus for the free world. If she keeps on speaking & writing her wish for a Free North Korea may come true in her lifetime.

Sirimavo Bandaranaike
(509)

Bandaranaike was born 17 April 1916 in Ceylon (*after 1972 Sri Lanka*); her mother was a physician and father was the 1st to receive British knighthood. At very young age she had access to her grandfather's literary & scientific library. She attended a private kindergarten, and went to Ferguson High School then to Catholic boarding school although was a practicing Buddhist throughout her life, Spoke fluent English and Sinhala; at 19 she organized clinics to improve life of village women. Her marriage was arranged but the first two suitors were rejected. She married Solomon Bandaranaike a wealthy lawyer & politician who served in the local State Council of Ceylon; both agreed to the marriage. Astrologers declared them compatible and married 2 Oct. 1940 in "the wedding of the century". For 20 years she devoted her time to raising the children, who were educated at Oxford, Paris, & London. She devoted herself to improve rice production, and was a key player in reducing India & China, tension. She met with delegates of Burma, Cambodia, Ghana, Ceylon, and the United Arab Republic. Nehru introduced her ideas to the Indian Parliament. Despite her success abroad she was criticized at home mostly for her ties with China. Some saw a drift toward Soviet Partnership. In Feb. 1964 Chinese Premier Zhou Enlai visited Bandaranaike with offers of Rice & textiles, and discussed border disputes. In 1964 she led a delegation to India and negotiated repatriation of the 975,000 stateless Tamils residing in Ceylon, and reached agreement granting citizenship to 300,000 Tamils, but now Ceylon faced a budget deficit of $195 million, caused by rising energy and declining revenue from coconut, rubber & tea export. In 1970 she traveled to Paris & London to discuss international trade, in that same year she ordered the Asia Foundation and the Peace Corps to leave, and granted recognition to East Germany, North Korea, & North Vietnam, but unemployment & inflation "*went south*". In 1971 her govt. was almost toppled by militants with attacks on the police station & US Embassy. She was loved around the world, but at home was another story. Discontented Tamils turned separatists. She was investigated for abuse of power, but kept her position as party leader making her prime minister, even though she was elected to that position after her husband was assassinated. She was expelled but retained her seat. In 1989 she survived a bombing attack in response to the killing of 30,000 to 70,000 rebels. In 1994 while suffering from diabetes she was confined to a wheelchair, and cited Health as the reason for stepping down. On 10 Oct, 2000 she died of a heart attack. Her marriage, as well as being one of the world's first woman prime ministers, helped break down centuries of social barriers. She was "*Mother of the People*" her children earned top political posts.

Vance Havner

(510)

Vance Havner was born 1901 in rural North Carolina US, 12 miles south of Hickory. His father was a potter at the wide spot in the road where he made and sold his ware; young Vance was an avid reader, even had some of his writings published in the local paper at age 10. He was teaching Sunday-School at age 9 in the local church, but was converted to Christianity at age 10, began preaching at age 12. Had no problem getting an audience, people came from all over to hear the boy preacher, his listeners often numbered just over 100, although he reached one time an audience of more than 1800. His only desire was to be a preacher being ordained at age 15. His written material from even the early days reveals a surprising level of maturity and understanding. He attended several colleges including Moody Bible Institute but never graduated from any. His mother church was the Southern Baptist Convention. When he was known to be in Charleston he was invited to speak at Citadel College where the chapel was filled to overflow capacity. (*During the 1960' and 70's I spent much time in the car and made sure I had all of Havner's cassette tapes with me; although I was in sales training and interested in motivation speakers, I purchased all the cassette tapes of Vance Havner that I could afford and listened to him on a daily basis.*) For several years he preached in town & country churches as a boy preacher, his sermons were published in newspaper columns they were eloquent and expressive. While in Florida at a college meeting, he met a young lady called Sara Allred, several years his junior; there were no sparks but a year later they met again and it was love and soon after in December 1940 and were married. She became an essential component of his itinerant ministry. When she died in 1973, he was emotionally devastated. As a preacher he gained a reputation as a homespun philosopher-humorist and was in demand as a preacher as well as an after-dinner speaker, he was entertaining and a man with a message from God. He was a revivalist focusing on stirring up the saints to a greater commitment, faithfulness, and service, rather than being an evangelist to the lost. His sphere of activity was primarily in the Southern states though he preached nearly in all the 50 states and conducted over 1,000 meetings. His sermons and speeches are down to earth, Bible centered, and powerful. His illustrations are incisive even when flavored with a touch of humor he maintained a love for the simple ways of his rural past. If there was a social gospel in the days of the prodigal son someone would have given him a bed and a sandwich and he would never go home. A medicine bottle often says Shake well before using. God often needs to do that before we are usable. Some preachers need to put fire in to their sermons but for some its better they put their sermons in the fire.

Ron Menor

(511)

Ron Menor was born in 1956 in Hawaii; the son of Hawaii State Supreme Court Justice Benjamin and Lillian Menor; Ron went to Iolani School, The University of California at Los Angeles and got his law degree from Georgetown University Law School; after that opened his own practice in Honolulu. Through an acquaintance Dr Quintin Uy (who introduced me to Ron), we discovered we were both new in business, Ron in <u>Law,</u> and I in <u>finance</u> and with advice of Hal Jones, Cam Cavasso, and a few others, Ron and I began a partnership of doing dinner or lunch seminars. We provided catered food, Ron offered legal counsel and I presented my financial pitch. We did that for about two years, although I also did that with 2 other attorneys such as Tyler Pottenger, and Scott Makuakani, it may not have been a great success but we needed to get our new business off the ground. We were all young and needed to start somewhere. Ron was great to work with as he was a driven man and most likely could have done well just in law with keen astute goals to serve the people of Hawaii; he was an ethical principled person and a member of Mililani Baptist Church. With the help of his father Justice Benjamin Menor he along with Dr Uy invited me to be a keynote speaker at the Philippine annual banquet, where many of the attendees were immigrants like we were. Justice Menor thanked me but I thought I was too young among all these professional people. In 1982 Ron set his heart on running for an elective office position in the Hawaii State Legislature; that was only the beginning, after a House seat it became the Senate and then the Honolulu City Council. I secretly hoped that all of that had begun in our living room but Ron was strong service driven and knew that I could not even take more than 1% credit for Ron's endeavors. Although we were both nondrinkers Ron did spent a night in jail for getting a DUI after a traffic stop even while his sons were with him in the car, he waited a few years and ran for office again; and proved that none of us is perfect, and Ron made a public apology. Elective office was in his blood he won and lost a few races. We were not members of the same political party but our friendship was never affected by that. Ron was a friend and had only one goal and that was to improve the lives in the community. When he was not in office, he was lobbying for things he believed in, especially issues that would make Hawaii a better place to live. For Ron to be a good public service was as natural as breathing. It was a major shock to read the newspaper headline that said: <u>Hawaii Politician Ron Menor died at age 67 on Monday 16 January 2023</u>. I was stunned to see Ron had not made it after an unexpected medical emergency, leaving behind his wife Pat and 3 sons. Ron was <u>not</u> a typical politician, he was a friend.

J. Gresham Machen

(512)

John Gresham Machen was born 28 July, 1881 in Baltimore Maryland US to Arthur Webster Machen and Mary Jones Gresham. Arthur was Episcopalian and Mary was Presbyterian and taught her son the Westminster Shorter Catechism from an early age. The family attended Franklin St. Presbyterian Church. Machen attended a private college and received a classical education including Latin and Greek and learned how to play the piano. In 1898 at age 17 he began his studies at Johns Hopkins University, and did so well, he got a scholarship. In school he was a brilliant student and majored in the classics. In 1901 he was elected to be a member of the Phi Beta Kappa Society after graduation. In 1902 he opted to study theology at Princeton Seminary, while simultaneously studying for a Master of Arts in philosophy at Princeton University. After graduation he became professor of New Testament at Princeton Seminary from 1906 to 1929 and led a revolt against modernist theology and formed Westminster Theological Seminary as a more orthodox alternative. As the Northern Presbyterian church continued to reject conservative attempts to enforce faithfulness to the Westminster Confession, Machen and a small group, formed the Orthodox Presbyterian Church. The Northern Church rejected his arguments and reorganized Princeton Seminary and created a liberal school. The Machen led a group formed Westminster Seminary in Philadelphia where he taught New Testament till he died in 1937. He is considered to be the last of the great Princeton Theologians who had developed the Princeton theology which was Conservative, Calvinist and Evangelical Christianity. Machen's influence can still be felt now through the existence of the institutions that he founded: <u>Westminster Theological Seminary</u>, <u>Independent Board of Foreign Missions</u>, and <u>The Orthodox Presbyterian Church</u>. In addition, his Greek textbook is still used today in many seminaries. Machen argued that liberalism is a form of disguised naturalism based on modernistic scientific theories and not on the Word of God. He declared that the Christian Religion is <u>*not*</u> the religion of the liberal church. In 1933 Machen withdrew from the Northern Presbyterian Church and formed the Orthodox Presbyterian Church. In his book *<u>The Great Evangelical Disaster</u>* Francis Schaeffer details the theological shift in American Christianity from conservatism to liberalism and says it was the culmination of a long trend toward liberalism within the Presbyterian Church which was the same trend in most other denominations. Machen was suspicious of mixing religion and politics. He opposed Prayer & Bible Reading in public schools, which implies that Christians should run their own schools. J. Gresham Machen died at age 55 on 1 January 1937 in Bismarck North Dakota, US.

Charles Stanley
(513)

Charles Frazier Stanley was born 25 Sept. 1932 in Dry Fork Virginia US. His father died before his first birthday; Charles grew up in rural Dry Fork area on the outskirts of Danville. At age 12 he was born again, at 14 he began working in Christian ministry, and obtained a bachelor's degree from the University of Richmond, a Master of Divinity from Southwestern Baptist Theological Seminary in Fort Worth Texas, as well as a Master of Theology and a Doctor of Ministry from Luther Rice Seminary in Florida, (*now located in Lithonia Georgia*). He joined the staff of First Baptist Church, Atlanta in 1969 and in 1971 became senior pastor. The ministry was a success and Stanley launched a TV program called <u>*The Chapel Hour.*</u> In 1977 founded television program <u>*In Touch Ministries*</u> with the mission to lead people worldwide into a growing relationship with Jesus Christ and to strengthen the local church. The Christian Broadcasting Network began televising <u>*In Touch*</u> in 1978. It has since been translated in 50 languages, is broadcast on 500 radio stations and 300 television stations and several satellite networks including the Inspiration Network along with other radio & video programming available on the In Touch Website. The ministry also publishes <u>*In Touch Magazine*</u> using tools like television, magazines, and digital media, to advance the

Gospel as quickly as possible. His writings address issues such as Finances, Parenting, Personal crisis, Emotional matters, Relationships, and Protestantism. His website unequivocally states that Dr Stanley fervently believes the Bible to be **The Inerrant Word of God**, a belief strongly reflected in all his teaching. In 1985 he was elected president of the Southern Baptist Convention. In 2020 at age 88 he announced his retirement as senior pastor, but made it clear that his work will continue. In 1992 his wife (*after 40 years of marriage*) filed for divorce, and both agreed to legally separate. It caused quite a controversy, but the members of his church overwhelmingly voted to keep him on as pastor as long as he did not remarry. He is an avid photographer, and much of his work is featured in the *In Touch Magazine* as well as in other materials printed by the ministry. Together they have a daughter named Becky and a son Andy who is a pastor at North Point Community Church in Georgia. Stanley invited Lisa Ryan to co-host a question-and-answer segment called "*Bring it Home*" which aired after his on-air sermons and is intended to answer questions the average listener may have. Ryan's participation ended in late 2006, but Stanley continued alone. He has lived by 30 life Principals; has written more than 45 books, hundreds of articles and broadcasts that continue to change the lives of millions every day; did he make a difference? May be more so then any other published here. Charles Stanley died of age 90 on 18 April, 2023.

Eddie Aikau

(514)

Edward Ryon Makuahanai Aikau was born on 5 May 1946 in Kahului, Maui, Hawaii. He was the 2nd child of Solomon & Henrietta Aikau and a descendant of Hewahewa the Kahuna Nui (*high priest*) of King Kamehameha-1. He learned how to surf on the shorebreak at Kahului Harbor. The family moved to Oahu in 1959 and Eddie left school to start working at Dole Pineapple Cannery. With money from his first paycheck, he bought a surfboard. In 1968 he became the first lifeguard hired by the City & County of Honolulu covering the beaches between Sunset and Haleiwa; he braved waves that often reached 30 ft (*9 meter*) and saved more than 500 swimmers, not one life was lost; With a record like that Eddie was named in 1971 "*Lifeguard of the year.*" In 1977 he won the Duke Kahanamoku Invitational Surfing Championship. On 28 Feb. 1978, TV producer John Orland was the last person Eddie rescued at Waimea Bay. In 1978 the Polynesian Voyaging Society was seeking volunteers for a 30-day, 2,500-mile (*4,000-km*) journey to re-enact the ancient route of the Polynesian migration between the Hawaiian and Tahitian island chains. Aikau joined the voyage as a crew member of the double-hulled voyaging canoe Hokule'a leaving the Hawaiian Islands on 16 March 1978. The canoe developed a leak in one of its hulls and capsized 12 miles (19 km) south of Moloka'i. Eddie in search for help, paddled on his surfboard toward Lana'i. The rest of the crew was rescued by the US Coastguard cutter Cape Corwin, but Eddie Aikau was never found and lost forever in the Pacific Ocean, his date of death is recorded as 17 March 1978. Eddie was only age 31 and considered to be one of the strongest swimmers. He had removed his life jacket since it was hindering his paddling of the surfboard. What followed was the largest air-sea-search in Hawaiian history, with no success. In his memory Quicksilver sponsored "*The Eddie*" at Sunset Beach in 1985 but cancelled, then re-opened. In the 1980's bumper stickers *Eddie Would Go* became popular. This year 2023 the *Big Wave Invitational* will include 6 women competing in waves as high as 50 feet; yesterday a rogue wave covered all beach spectators and sucked 2 adults and a baby into the ocean, life guards were able to rescue all. The wave came out of nowhere and caught unsuspecting spectators by surprise thinking they were safe. It is a dangerous and risky endeavor to be near the beach with 50 ft waves. We have lived here over 60 years and our children work as lifeguards and gained a healthy respect for the ocean. Every day the whaling sirens go past our home and on a few occasions some of our close friends were the victims and did not make it.

Eva Peron

(515)

Maria Eva Duarte de Peron was born most likely as an illegitimate child on 7 May 1919 in Argentina. Her childhood is a little mysterious, although she was filled with passion and combativeness. There are innuendos of forged birth, and marriage certificates. She was born in poverty in a rural village of Argentina and was given the nickname of *Evita*. At age 15 she moved to the nation's capital Buenos Aires to pursue a career as a film actress and work in radio. In 1944 she met Colonel Juan Peron at a charity event for earthquake victims. They were married in 1945 and Juan Peron was elected President of Argentina in 1946. Eva was a powerful woman speaking for labor rights, even became the pro-Peronist party leader running the Ministries of Labor & Health. She founded the Eva Peron Foundation, championed women's suffrage, and ran the nation's first large-scale Female Peronist Party. With that strong support, Juan Peron won 63% of the vote in the 1951 presidential election. He then chose Eva as a candidate for vice president, meaning should he die she would be president. She became immensely popular among the working class so much so, it even surprised her husband, especially when he saw her popularity equaled his. At a very large rally in 1951 while standing under the largest photo of her & Juan Peron she declined the invitation to be Vice

President. The year before she had fainted in a public meeting and underwent surgery 3 days later. It was reported she had an appendectomy but in fact had been diagnosed with advanced cervical cancer, and her health was rapidly declining. In 1952 on her 33rd birthday the Argentine Congress pronounced her the "*Spiritual Leader of the Nation*" by. On 4 June 1952 Evita rode next to her husband in a victory celebration parade but was to sick to finish and returned home, taking a triple dose of her medication, but the cancer metastasized and she was the first Argentine to undergo chemotherapy, (*a novel treatment at that time*), but her weight rapidly dropped to 79 lbs. On 26 July 1952 radio broadcasts throughout Argentina were interrupted, advising that their beloved Spiritual Leader Eva (*Evita Peron*) had died, the government suspended all official activities. Her body was laid in State at the Ministry of Labor, and later in Congress. The streets in Buenos Ares overflowed with flowers, all shops sold out. She was the first person who never held office, to be given a State Funeral usually reserved for a head of state. Her body was laid in state, first at the ministry of labor, then at Congress, and following that it was placed on a gun carriage pulled by government officials through the streets while flowers were thrown from balconies. Eva Peron began her life as a peasant girl and died as a queen at only age 30 or 33.

R. C. Sproul

(516)

Robert Charles Sproul was born 13 Feb.1939, In Pittsburgh Pennsylvania US. At age 15 he had to drop out from high-school-athletics in order to support the family. He obtained degrees from Westminster College (BA 1961), Pittsburgh Theological Seminary (MDiv, 1964) Free University Amsterdam (Drs. 1969), and Whitefield Theological Seminary (PhD, 2001). Sproul taught at numerous colleges and seminaries, including the Reformed Theological Seminary in Orlando, and in Jackson Mississippi and Knox Theological Seminary in Ft Lauderdale. One of his mentors was John Gerstner, professor at Pittsburg-Xenia Theological Seminary who along with another of Gerstner students Arthur Lindsley, Coauthored the book <u>Classical Apologetics</u> in 1984. (An interesting note here is that some time ago I had an open day between 2 seminars in Geneva and Art's wife Connie and Jamal Hashway from Jordan and 2 others suggested we do a little sightseeing in Switzerland. We did so and toured all the historical places around Geneva; it was not an official meeting day but it was one the highlights of the entire trip). Sproul married Vesta Voorhis in 1960 and they had 2 children Sherrie and Robert. Sproul for some reason did not care to fly and avoided airplanes as much as he could and would travel by car, train, boat or Bus. He was a passenger on the Amtrak Train en route from Los Angeles to Miami when on 22 Sept. 1993 at 2.45 AM, with 220 passengers & crew aboard, while crossing the <u>Big Bayou Cannot Bridge</u> in Alabama, derailed, crashed, and plunged in the water, 103 were injured and 48 people died, by <u>drowning, fire</u> or <u>smoke inhalation</u>, although Sproul survived that accident. Ligonier Ministries hosts several theological conferees each year and is the primary organization that continues what he begun. He served as co-pastor at St Andrew's Chapel in Sanford Florida. Sproul was ordained as an elder in the United Presbyterian Church in America in 1965, but left the denomination in 1975 and joined the Presb. Church in America. He was an advocate of Calvinism, which is the dominant theme in *<u>Renewing Your Mind</u>* lessens where it is clear that God's holiness and sovereignty are supreme. In 2015 RC suffered a stroke but 5 days later on 23 April 2015 he was home again with his family. He was a longtime heavy cigarette smoker and on 14 December 2017 at the age of 78, RC Sproul died. He left behind many books and articles where he explained complicated theological issues in simple to understand language. <u>His teaching was below seminary but above Sunday- School</u>. With the help of Ligonier Ministries his *<u>down-to-earth</u>* instruction continues to reach millions in multi languages around the world.

Arthur Lindsley

(517)

Arthur Lindsley earned his Bachelor of Science in Chemistry from Seattle Pacific University, and is, (_or was_) scholar-in-residence at the C. S. Lewis Institute in Virginia since 1987. He holds a B. A. from Seattle Pacific Univ. an MDiv from Pittsburgh Theological Seminary, and a Ph.D. from the University of Pittsburgh. He is co-author of <u>Classical Apologetics</u> with Dr. R.C. Sproul, and Dr. John Gerstner. Formerly he was the director of Educational Ministries at Ligonier Valley Study Center. Dr. Lindsley is on the staff of 4th Presb. Church in Metropolitan Wash. D.C. where he teaches classes. (_My friend Ken Carlson was an organist there during the years of Richard Halverson, it was the church I usually visit when in DC_). Lindsley also taught at the Natl. Presbyterian Church, teaching preparation classes for <u>Young Life</u> each year and speaks at conferences throughout the US and the world. Dr. Lindsley is the author of C.S. Lewis's "<u>Case for Christ, Love, True Truth</u>, and has written numerous articles on apologetics, on theology, and the lives & works of many authors and teachers. He is Vice President and teaches Theological Initiatives at the Institute for Faith & Economics where he oversees the development of a theology that integrates faith, work, and economics. He is also co-founder of Reformed Theological Seminary's Wash. D.C. Campus, and is editor and contributing author of *Institute for Faith, Works & Economics* (IFWE0's *Counting the Cost: Christian Perspective on Capitalism* (Abelene Christian University Press, 2017) and *For the Least of These*, a Biblical answer to Poverty (Zondervan, (2015). Dr Lindsey's key research in these books deal with two Biblical passages commonly used to promote socialism: *Leviticus 25* and the topic of Jubilee, and *Acts 2-5*. In one of his books he writes: "*Conventional wisdom holds that any belief in absolutes, especially of a religious nature, leads inevitably to the oppressive absolutism of such movements as the Inquisition, the Crusades and even Nazism. As a result Christian Apologetics have been hard pressed to make a case for the rational absolutes that are a necessary part of belief in Jesus. He takes up that task in The Truth a book that defends absolutism in a relativistic world. (*We met in Geneva at a Global Hope conference, during a free day between meetings; I had just returned from China, was tired & planning to sleep. But Jamal from Jordan said: Terry I'm not going to let u sleep we are going to find 4 people and go site-seeing. He found Connie Lindsley, me, and a local lady with a car. That was supposed to be a "*sitting in my room day*"; it turned out to be one of the high-lights of *that* Geneva trip.) Since then lost contact for 10 yrs and just renewed our friendship by phone. Dr Lindsley and his wife Connie & 2 sons live in Arlington VA; they are people of *class* and a joy to be with.

Allan Bakke

(518)

Allan Bakke was a U.S. Marine Captain and had served in Vietnam as well as a NASA engineer, applied for a position in medical school at age 35 and tested with scores of 96th, 94th, 97th and 72nd percentiles. Despite outstanding qualifications and consideration that should have been given to him as a veteran, Bakke was rejected not once but twice. The medical school accepted 100 students each year and set aside 16 slots for minorities. Bakke learned that lesser qualified had been admitted in preference to him with test scores in the 34th, 30th, 37th, and 18th percentiles. He sued the Regents of the Univ. of California stating that minority applicants were accepted. His Civil Rights discrimination grievance reached the US Supreme Court in 1978 at a time when black schoolchildren were bussed to schools not in their neighborhood, and Civil Rights legislation was introduced intending to give blacks more power. It was in that environment that The US Supreme Court ruled about the Bakke case on 28 June 1978 & declared affirmative action constitutional but invalidated the use of racial quotas. The medical School at the University of California, Davis, (as part of the university's affirmative action program), had reserved 16 percent of its admission places for minority applicant. Allan Bakke, a white California man had twice unsuccessfully applied for admission to the medical school filed suit against the University citing evidence that his grades and test scores surpassed those of many minority students who had been accepted for admission, Bakke charged that he had suffered unfair reverse discrimination on the basis of race; he argued his case was contrary to the Civil Rights Act of 1964 and the equal protection clause of the US Constitution's Fourteenth Amendment. The Supreme Court, in a highly fractured ruling, (*six separate opinions were issued*), agreed that the university's use of strict racial quotas was unconstitutional and ordered that the medical school admit Bakke and said that the University had erred in creating an impermissible quota. But the court, then in a convoluted statement, said that while quotas were impermissible, race may be one of the many factors that could be considered in admissions decisions of institutions of higher education. Although the ruling legalized the use of affirmative action which is the glorified policy of liberal Democrats, in subsequent decisions during the next several decades the court limited the scope of such programs, and several U.S. states prohibited affirmative action programs based on race. We suggest, (considering that issue), if u spent 5 min. reading about academic decisions you should be as confused as we were. Bakke finished medical school and became an anesthesiologist.

Vishal Mangalwadi

(519)

Vishal Mangalwadi was born 20 Dec. 1949 in Vindhya Pradesh, India; he grew up along with 6 siblings in the States of Utter Pradesh India and graduated from the University of Allahabad in 1969, earned an MA in philosophy from the University of Indore in 1973. In 1974 Mangalwadi co-founded The Theological Research and Communication Institute (TRACI) and began to develop a master's thesis which became his first book, *The World of Gurus*. In 1975 He married Ruth a graduate of Lucknow University who returned to India after obtaining a master's degree in theology from Wheaton College in Illinois US in 1976, they moved to his father's farm in Getheora village in Chhatarpur District; founded a non-profit organization *Association for Comprehensive Rural Assistance* (ACRA) to serve the rural poor and transform their caste-based feudal social system. His work was opposed and violently resisted. In 1980 Vishal was briefly incarcerated in Tikamgarh Jail where he began writing his book, *Truth and Social Reform*. During the anti-Sikh riots that followed the assassination of Prime Minister Indira Gandhi in 1984, his structure was also burned down. From 1984 to 1987 Mangalwadi was the honorary director of TRACI and published *Truth & Social Reform*. In 1984, he was appointed Convener of the Peasant's Commission of the Janata Party. In 1987, he initiated a national movement against revival of sati. From 1988 to 1994 he was an assistant to Kanshiram, the founder of the Bahujan Samaj Party. Since 1996 he has been writing lecturing, and publishing around the world. In 2003, William Carey International University awarded him a Doctorate in Laws. In 2009 he published the US edition of Truth and Transformation, encouraging local churches around the world to promote this vision of church and internet based higher education and has been institutionalized in two organizations: Church and Community Centered Higher Education, *CACHE* Virtues Inc is implementing the concept in the USA. He writes regularly for the New-Delhi based bi-lingual monthly FORWARD Press. He served as Honorary Professor of Applied Theology and the Director of Centre for Human Resource Development at Sam Higginbottom University of Agriculture, Technology & Sciences. In January of 2009 he lectured in our home for two days here in Hawaii with an attendance of 84 seated theater style in the large front room from 9 AM to 5 PM with coffee and lunch breaks. Vishal Mangalwadi is a Social Reformer, Political columnist, Christian Philosopher, Writer, Lecturer, and is Indian-American. After the seminar Vishal & Ruth stayed with us for a two week R & R. A year later we were in California and stayed at their home. Many of the books continue his endeavors for years to come.

Ludwig II of Bavaria

(520)

Ludwig Otto Friedrich Wilhelm was born 25 Aug. 1845 in the Palace in Central Munich; he was the elder son of Maximilian II of Bavaria and Marie of Prussia, and did not enjoy an ideal childhood, his parents were distant, although Ludwig ascended to the Bavarian throne in 1864 at the age of 18. When he appeared at his father's funeral, he was virtually unknown. His spectacular good looks, and regal, made deep impression on his subjects making him instantly popular. Two years later, Bavaria & Austria, fought a war against Prussia and lost. In 1870 Bavaria sided with Prussia in their successful war against France. Then Bavaria <u>& 21 other monarchies</u> became part of the new <u>German Empire</u> (<u>*Deutsche Reich*</u>) in 1871. Ludwig felt emasculated as a ruler and increasingly withdrew from day-to-day-affairs-of-state in favor of his artistic architectural project which he eventually commissioned as the new palace, and is now known to us as the most famous <u>Neuschwanstein Castle</u>. He was also a devoted patron of the composer Richard Wagner. His extravaganza was used against him to declare him insane, (*an accusation that has since come under scrutiny*), although it earned him the various titles of Moon king, or Mad King. (Put some royalty in the mix and you have a mystery story). Ludwig was taken in to custody on 12 June 1886; the following day he and his doctor were found dead in the lake, it was ruled suicide, (it too was *disputed*). Neuschwanstein embodies both the contemporaneous architectural fashion known as castle-romanticism or as said in Deutschland *Burgenromantik*. Opera fans can detect the king's enthusiasm of <u>*Tannhauser*</u> and <u>*Lohengrin*</u>, <u>(operas of Richard Wagner)</u>, in the final design. On some of our European safaris we likely saw as many castles as Thailand has temples. Many of these castles were constructed and re-constructed to make them more picturesque, subsequently most architects and designers never saw the (<u>*no pun intended*</u>) <u>product of their conception</u>. The world remembers Ludwig for his fairytale castle, immortalized by Walt Disney as the *Sleeping Beauty Palace* although it was not the only castle Ludwig built; his ministers were mad as hornets about the fact that costs were repeatedly revised worrying the country would be bankrupted over the king's pet project, his dream fortress. The castle was representing a romantic era of the middle ages, as well as the musical mythology of his friend Wagner, whose operas had made a lasting impression on him. Despite its size the castle did not have space for the royal court. The king's wishes and demands expended well beyond the cost. In 1880 about 200 craftsmen were occupied at the site. The king's extravagant 19th century Neuschwanstein Castle stands on a rugged hill above the village Hohenschwangau in southwest Bavaria; Ludwig II died 13 June 1886.

Ernest Cassutto

(521)

Ernest Cassutto was born 1 December 1919 in Probolinggo East Indies (*now Indonesia*), the middle son of secular Jewish parents; He had a brother called George and a sister Hetty. Their father was a law professor and the family settled in The Hague (*Den Haag*) in the Netherlands in 1934. Despite Dutch neutrality and empty promises from Hitler, Nazi Germany invaded Holland on 10 May 1940, and bombed the civilian population in Rotterdam & Den Haag. Ernest was captured and imprisoned in Rotterdam. While he was hiding in Rotterdam a friend came to him and said: Ernie, I have some bad news; your fiancé has been arrested. Ernest was not unable to process that and slumped to the floor crying out loud "*I am all alone*" but that was not all, a few years later he discovered that his fiancé was sent to a concentration camp and was killed; it was almost more than he could handle. Ernest was rescued by a Dutch Christian underground worker who was later executed by the Nazis as the war came to a close. During captivity, Ernest began writing about his experiences in World War II; a riveting story that speaks of horror, but also radiates the love of God. Later he had his war episodes published in a book titled: *The Last Jew of Rotterdam*, which was originally released by Whitaker House. In no time the book was out of print, but due to continued interest, his story, was re-written and updated by his son, Dr Benjamin H. Cassutto. The newer version of the book was released by Purple Pomegranate Productions. Another son, George H. Cassutto wrote & maintains a website. Ernest became a minister in the Reformed Church and immigrated to America in 1952 under the auspices of the Hebrew Christian Alliance and the Reformed Church of America. He settled in the United States with his wife and fellow Holocaust survivor Elisabeth and their infant daughter. Ernest was a minister-at-large in the North Jersey-New York metropolitan area. In 1968 he became the pastor of Emmanuel Hebrew Christian Church in Villa Nova Baltimore County, until his retirement in 1979. The book is a study of the life of Ernest Cassutto and his transition from agnosticism to Christianity along with the turbulence of the world around him. It is the story of a man who survived the most difficult situation and managed to float above the seas of time because God gave him supernatural strength; it covers the same time as that of the _Diary of Anne Frank._ If you read _The Last Jew of Rotterdam_, you will be blessed it is a captivating story and is one of those that you can not put it down until you get to page 171. Although I lived through that same war his perspective was striking. Ernest Cassutto died at age 66 in Baltimore on 18 March 1985.

Ann Coulter

(522)

Ann Coulter was born Dec. 8, 1961 in New York City, to John V. Coulter an FBI agent from a working class Catholic Irish, American, and German family, and her mother's ancestry was traced to the puritan settlers in the Plymouth Colony. She has 2 older brothers James & John; the family moved to Connecticut where Ann graduated from New Canaan High School in 1980 and went on to Cornell University where she helped found the *Cornell Review* and was a member of the Delta Gamma national sorority. She graduated cum laude from Cornel in 1984 with a Bachelor of Arts in history and a Juris Doctor from the University of Michigan Law School in 1988 where she was the editor of the Michigan Law Review. Her Birth date was disputed and it was asserted that she was born in 1963 not 1961. After Law School she served as clerk for a judge in the U.S. Court of Appeals for the 8th circuit. She publishes a syndicated newspaper column and her style has often been labeled of being polemic. She certainly has not been shy of stirring controversy. At one of her Q&A sessions in Indiana a student asked "*Are you guided by your religion, or how her religion guides her political opinions.*" To which she responded: *Do you think I'm mean*, and before she finished her answer, Ann walked off the stage; amidst a mix of claps, boos, and chants of "*Let her finish*" as attendees filed out of the auditorium. Ann is the author of twelve books. In 2010 it was estimated that she has made about $500,000 on the speaking circuit giving speeches on such topics as *Modern Conservatism, Gay Marriage* which she describes as the hypocrisy of modern American liberalism, During one appearance at the University of Arizona, a pie was thrown at her. She has written about such topics as *High Crimes and Misdemeanors, the case against Bill Clinton, Liberal lies about American Right, Treason, How to talk to a Liberal, If Democrat had any brains, They'd be Republicans, How the Liberal Mob is endangering America, Racial Demagoguery from the seventies to Obama, Never trust a liberal, Adios America, The left's plan to turn our country into a Third World Hellhole. Godless: The church of Liberalism,* Some papers dropped her column especially when it came to the point that she was the issue, rather then what she was writing about. I am a fan of her writings end though her logic is often devastating, her viewpoints are right most of the time. She makes appearance on radio and TV. She is a Presbyterian a conservative is pro-life and has been opposed to the 1973 Supreme Court decision on abortion. She is opposed to same sex marriage. Ann has never been married although been engaged several times but is single and has no children. She has lived in New York, California, and Florida, and votes in Palm Beach Fl.

Maria Bartiromo

(523)

Maria Sara Bartiromo was born 11 September 1967 to Italian-American parents Vincent and Josephine Bartiromo and was raised in Brooklyn in New York City, US. Her father was a restaurant owner, and she served as the hostess seating people. She attended Fontbonne Hall Academy; an all girl's private Catholic School, while working as a coat check person at her parent's restaurant. She became a stock clerk at Kleinfeld's wedding dress shop; there was fired for trying-on the newly arrived dresses before putting them away. She recalled I cried the whole way home, but learned a valuable lesson, – do your job. She got an internship on Barry Farber's show on WMCA 570 in New York. In 1993 she was hired by Roger Ailes to work at CNBC and began reporting live from the floor at the New York Sock Exchange, as well as hosting and contributing to *the Market Watch* and *Squawk Box segments*. She was the first journalist to deliver life television reports from the raucous floor of New York Stock Exchange. *The Guardian* reported: her 5 ft 5 frame was jostled by burly traders, but Maria became influential with the Financial Times who called her the Sofia Loren of Wall Street. She has appeared on *The Tonight Show* with Jay Leno, on CBS with *Oprah Winfrey* and has guest hosted on the syndicated *Live with Regis and Kelly*. She has been nicknamed *the Money Honey* in the 1990's and had conflicted feelings about that, lest it diminished her credibility as a financial journalist. She anchored the television coverage of New York City's Columbus Day Parade beginning 1995 and was the Grand Marshal in 2010. She has been criticized about journalistic integrity, but NBC upper management had full confidence in Maria and said her scrupulous principles were never compromised. When in 2008 some Wall Street firms collapsed Bartiromo commented: "I'm a free market capitalist who would like to think that the market can correct itself, although the structures we have in place dropped the ball, and boards of directors were asleep at the wheel, so were the regulators. After Trump came in office she was an advocate repeating administration talking points. In Nov.2020 she conducted the first post-election interview with Trump and was criticized for that. She complained to Atty general Bill Barr that the DOJ did nothing to stop Democrats from stealing the election. Maria was outspoken about the fact that election machines were rigged, so did Lou Dobbs & Jeanine Pirro. Maria received the excellence in broadcast Journalism Award, along with many others. In 1999 she married Jonathan Steinberg, son of billionaire Saul Steinberg, they met in 1990. Maria Bartiromo is one of the finest financial reporters anywhere and for full disclosure; I owned a financial business for 45 years.

Klaas Runia

(524)

Klaas Runia was born 7 May 1926 in Oudeschoot, Heerenveen municipality, Friesland, the Netherlands. He grew up as child in Friesland and studied at the Free University of Amsterdam. Upon graduation he became eligible to preach and his first sermons in the Gereformeerde Kerk, (*Reformed Church*) became a phenomenal success. Not common for new aspiring preachers, but he received from 20 to 25 calls in his first year, and was the most sought after candidate; but he felt the Lord led him in other directions and accepted the call to a very small church that could not afford him, nor had a place for him to live. This allowed him to continue his studies toward a doctorate with a dissertation on the concept of theological time in Karl Bart 1955; then as a young man with his earned doctorate in theology, he was asked to become professor of Systematic theology at the Reformed Theological Seminary in Geelong, Australia, which he accepted and became the Dean of the College teaching there until 1970. (My brother in law was one of his students in that seminary, and later took his place). Dr Runia exerted much influence on Evangelicals in the churches, the universities, and theological schools, of all of New Zealand and Australia. When he left there he made an R&R stop in our home in Honolulu. His signature in our guest book is dated 22 Sept. 1970 staying with his wife for 1 or 2 days, on the way back to the Netherlands. He was much too young to retire, and kept writing scholarly books and articles in multi languages. Upon his return in Europe, he was elected chairman of the Reformed Ecumenical Council till 1976. In 1971 he was appointed Professor of Practical Theology at the Kampen Theological University. During his professorship he was heavily engaged in church affairs and regarded as a leader of the orthodox wing of the Reformed Church (Gereformeerde Kerken van Nederland), now changed to: *the Protestant Church in the Netherlands*). For many years he was active as a journalist and was editor-in-chief of *Centraal Weekblad* from 1972 to 1996. He wrote many articles in the Frisian daily newspapers, specifically *the Friesch Dagblad*. He retired in 1992, but remained active as a theologian and journalist until his death... Much of his works are still available in book-form, in several languages. *Karl Barth's Doctrine of Holy Scripture*, 1962 ; *I Believe in God*, 1963; *Reformation Today*, 1968; *The sermon under attack*, 1983; *The present day Christological debate*, 1984; and many more; some are not in the English language, such as *Wegen & Doolwegen*, 1982, (*new theology or Right Road and Wrong Road*). Dr Klaas Runia died at age 80 on 14 October 2006 in Kampen the Netherlands and left large footprints, especially for young aspireing preachers.

Gabby Pahinui
(525)

Charles Kapono Kahahawai Jr. Pahinui was born 22 April 1921 in Honolulu Hawaii, into a struggling family, and later hanaied with his brother and one of his sisters to Philip and Emily Pahinui was raised in the impoverished district of Kaka'ako in Honolulu in the 1920's, ("*all tin roofs and kinda falling apart.*") He took the name of Philip Kunia Pahinui and spent his childhood supporting the family selling newspapers and shining shoes. He attended Pohukaina School but dropped out after 5th grade. In 1938 he married Emily Pulipuli at age 17, she was 19; together they had 12 children 6 boys and 6 girls and remained married until his death. He landed a job as a backup guitarist and mastered the steel guitar (*kika kila*), even learned to read music. At that time most musicians only played in bars. Gabby is known for his mastery of the traditional Hawaiian slack key guitar (Ki Ho'alu key slackened downtuned, usually to an open-string chord with low bass notes, then finger picked), and his beautiful expressive vocals. Gabby learned slack-key from Herman Keawe, whom Gabby acknowledges as being "the greatest slack-key player of all time." Herman, like Gabby, lived in the Kaka'ako area. In 1946 Gabby made his first recording "Hi'ilawe" for the Bell Records label. It is believed to be the first record of a Hawaiian song with slack-key guitar and it inspired many local musicians. The following year came "Hula Medley" the first record of a slack-key guitar instrumental, and that was inducted into the US National recording Registry for cultural historical or aesthetical significance. Gabby played with many of the great bands and musicians of his time, including Lena Machado and Ray Kinney. He appeared on *Hawaii Calls*, a popular international radio show that began in the 1930's. Eventually, Gabby moved his wife & family to Waimanalo, which had become a second home for a number of Hawaii musicians. The all-weekend jam sessions at the Pahinui home became legendary. Despite his success, Gabby still had financial trouble, and worked for City & County road crews doing pick & shovel work. The Hawaiian Renaissance of the 1970's launched a cultural reawakening of all things Hawaiian; Gabby played a very important part in that. In 1972 he made four albums with what came to be called the "*Gabby Band*", in there his four sons were featured. Gabby received the Hawaiian Academy of Recording Artists Lifetime Achievement Award in 1997, and was inducted into the Hawaiian Music Hall of Fame in 2002. All his children are active in Music, although his son Philip chose not to pursue it professionally. Gabby Pahinui died of a heart attack on 13 October 1980, at age 59 and has inspired thousands of children who learned that they were worthy as a people.

Michelle Wie

(526)

Michelle Sung Wie was born 11 October 1989 in Honolulu Hawaii and went to Punahou School. Upon graduation in 2006 she announced that she had set her sights on Stanford University. She completed her studies in 2012 with a major in communication. Wie began playing golf at the age of four, and at ten she became the youngest player ever to qualify for the Women Amateur Public Links Championship. On 5 October, 2005, a week before her 16th birthday Wie announced she was turning professional, and had signed sponsorship contracts with Nike and Sony valued at more than $10 million a year. She could not be a member of a professional tour, LPGA age requirements is 18. She asked for an age exemption but that was denied. She played her first professional event in 2005 LPGA Samsung World Championship, where she was disqualified for signing an incorrect scorecard. In May 2006 she became first female medalist in a local qualifier for the men's US Open, but did not advance; she withdrew from the tour citing heat exhaustion and tiredness. Wie played on European and Asian tours, and became the 2nd woman (after Se Ri Pak) to make the cut on the Asian Tour, and in addition, reportedly received appearance fees exceeding the events total prize money. However, she finished the season with several disappointing performances in both male and female tournaments, including the Omega European Masters, PGA84 Lumber Classic, LPGA Tour Samsung World Championship ad the Casio World Open. At this point Wie had played 14 Consecutive rounds of tournament golf without breaking par and had missed the cut in 11 out of 12 tries against men and remained winless against the women. In 2007 Wie's slump continued including a four-month hiatus, due to injuries in wrists, a disqualification and several missed cuts and withdrawals. The LPGA rule of 88, states that a non-LPGA member shooting a score of 88 or more is forced to withdraw and banned from LPGA co-sponsored events for the rest of the year. Despite the lack of victories, Wie was ranked #4 in the 2007 Forbes Top 20 Earners under 25, with annual earnings of $19 million, and finally became eligible to play full-time on the LPGA Tour in 2009 when she tied for 7th place at the qualifying tournament in Daytona Beach. In 2006 Wie was a captain's pick for the US team in Solheim Cup competition where she led the American squad to victory with a 3-0-1 performance the best record on the American team. Wie married Jonnie West in 2019 and together they have one child. In 2020 she contributed to CBS Sports. Wie has traveled the world with win's and losses, victories & defeats, but she has lived a life doing what she loved.

Chloe Cole

(527)

Chloe Cole was (in our opinion) abused and misrepresented by people who willfully neglected their adult duties to provide a teenager with care & guidance that has existed since the dawn of civil societies, but was neglected by those who could protect her from harming herself. Learned people of questionable mind did not carry out their "<u>*parental adult*</u>" wisdom but stood by, even participated, to let a teenager destroy herself by suicide or mutilation. Last years' TV program "<u>Teens against Gender Mutilation Rally</u>," featured Chloe Cole as keynote speaker, she described the <u>Trans Community</u> as "a cult" and spoke against gender affirming care for minors, she favored a bill that would <u>*ban*</u> gender-affirming surgeries for minors. *Why is there even a need for such legislation?* On 9 Nov. 2022 Chloe (being represented by Atty Harmeet Dhillon) filed a 90-day notice of intent to sue against the healthcare company Kaiser Permanente, the endocrinologist, the psychiatrist and the plastic surgeon involved in Cole's treatment, all of whom should know better; it should include her high School counselors, and her parents, (if they were aware). She had a double mastectomy at age 15; because she thought she should be a boy, even though the hormones God gave her will always be female and never become male, meaning she has been assisted by adults of the far left who put this young girl on an irreversible road of high probability leading to suicide. After the damage was done, she expressed regret and was offered breast reconstruction surgery which understandably she turned down. What is a big puzzle; most sane individuals will stop anyone from self-destruction, in these cases doctors & social workers encouraged and participated when this child mutilated herself and help her do irreversible damage, all done at an age too young to buy a beer. Such doctors need to be removed from endangering these young people and (just like their victims, whom they have robbed of a normal life forever), should have their license removed with no reinstatement, they do not belong in the healing profession; but are a danger to society. Young people often do crazy things but as a rule generally come through it and grow up. That's why common sense has dictated age restrictions to protect children. I came here as a Hitler survivor and have studied the camp doctors of Auschwitz who experimented with the most evil practices; some of them were tried at Nuremberg and received their just rewards, although all said "*Hitler made me do it*". I chose to come here after America victoriously won a war on 2 fronts. We have now plunged headlong in a Godless society more evil then Hitler and his minions. I am aware of Pol-Pot, Joseph Stalin, Idi Amin, and others; but this is America, more blest by God than any other and now we are marching back to such satanic evil, is that what we want?

Frank Pavone

(528)

Frank Anthony Pavone was born 4 February 1959 in Port Chester, New York to Joseph and Marion Pavone. His father was a hardware salesman. At a very young age he decided to become a priest. He attended the 1976 March for life, although the attendance was primarily Catholic people; I attended that same March and we met there. Frank enrolled at the Bosco College, a Salesian major seminary in Newton, New Jersey, later leaving that order and joined the Archdiocese of New York, where he was ordained to the priesthood on 12 Nov. 1988 by another personal friend: Cardinal John O'Connor then Archbishop of New York, and was assigned to St Charles Church Staten Island. During that time, in addition to parish duties, he began producing television broadcasts on local cable TV channels. In 1993, he sought and obtained permission from O'Connor to devote his ministry to ending abortion, and O'Connor appointed his as director of *Priests for Life*.

In the late 1990's, Pavone served at the Holy See's Pontifical Council for the Family, and coordinated pro-life activities for the Catholic Church world-wide, he encouraged pro-life leaders to establish local projects. The National Right to Life Committee honored him for unselfish help to Pro Life organization and hosted Fr Pavone at the Waldorf-

Astoria hotel in New York. After a difference of opinion with Cardinal Edward Egan in New York, he sought & received transfer to Amarillo Texas. There the diocese announced that he would establish Missionaries of the Gospel of Life. Then Pavone indicated that Priests for Life and Missionaries of the Gospel of Life were interfering with his work. In 2001 Pavone announced a $12 million advertising campaign designed to welcome women who had abortions back into the church. Due to a series of disagreements, he was dismissed from the priesthood and laicized for disobedience of lawful instructions of his bishop. When contacted in December 2022 and asked about it he told catholic news agency: *This is the first time I heard about it.* A spokesman for his team said Pavone continued to celebrate Mass and he is a member in good standing. As far as we can determine his dismissal has no moral or criminal implication, but has been primary over disagreements with some of his bishops about internal church issues. Therefore, considering the volume of work he has done on behalf of the babies, we see no reason he should not be on these pages. Having worked alongside of him on few issues there are none that we can think of who are more committed to truth as he is. The prefect of the Dicastery for the Clergy wrote a letter in November 2022 explaining that the decision to dismiss him is not open for appeal. We will not judge here, but will honor him for his dedication to God and the unborn.

Gerard Van Groningen

(529)

Gerard Van Groningen was born on 25 March 1921 in Leota Minnesota to Hendrick & Jennie Van Groningen. The family moved to California where he was raised in Ripon Calif. After serving in the US Armed forces in Japan during WW-II, he studied for the ministry at Calvin College and Seminary graduating in 1954. Westminster Seminary in Philadelphia awarded him a ThM degree in 1955. He started his ministry in Borculo Christian Reformed Church in Zeeland Michigan US and taught classes at Covenant Seminary in St Louis Mo. From there he went to Victoria Australia and became one of the founding professors of the Geelong Reformed Seminary. While there, he took classes at the University of Melbourne and attained his doctorate in philosophy in 1968. While teaching at the Australian Seminary, (*my brother-in-law who was one of his students*), told me that he was always available for help, to prove that, he never closed his office door, leaving it wide open for any student to walk in who wanted help or was struggling with questions. He was influential in the early stages of Reformed Theological education in Latvia and Brazil and on two separate occasions he served as seminary planter there;. The Reformed churches of a number of countries have richly profited from his teachings. One time in 1969 we visited family in New Zealand at the same time Van Groningen was the guest speaker at the church in Hamilton, New Zealand. He preached a very powerful sermon and the closing song was the familiar hymn authored by Frances R. Havergal titled "*Take my life and let it be*, where the 4th verse read *Take my silver and my gold, not a mite will I withhold;*" And in the middle of the song he jumped to his feet and shouted *STOP, STOP, STOP* with microphone in hand walked among the pews, intently looking at each person, asking: Did you mean what you just sung? *Take my silver and my gold, not a mite will I withhold?* If you did, please continue singing the hymn, if not, please sit down. Perhaps a little theatrical but ever since I look a lot closer at the words when we sing. He finished his teaching position in Australia and traveled through Honolulu made an R&R stop at our home, according to the guest book he stayed a few days on 22 March 1971, and moved on to Iowa where he served as professor of Bible at Dordt College teaching Old Testament. He served as president of Trinity Christian College from 1980 to 1984 and later as Adjunct Professor Emeritus at Covenant Theological Seminary from 1985. He married Harriet Stuitje in 1949 and they were together 64 years and had 8 children, 34 Grandchildren, and 29 great grand-children. Gerard Van Groningen died at age 93 on 20 June 2014; he left numerous theological, articles and sermons, he authored 10 theological books. He gave u the feeling he was a lifelong brother, I miss him.

Marko Kropyvnytskyi

(530)

Marko Kropyvnytskyi was born 7 May 1840 in Bezhbairaky in Russian Empire, now named Kropyvnytskyi in his honor and is part of Ukraine. He was a Ukrainian writer, dramaturge, composer, theatre actor, and director. Over his career he wrote more than 40 plays, played in over 500 roles of various repertoires, as well as wrote several songs. In 1875 he was invited by Theophilia Romanovich to the theatrical society "*Ruska Besida*" he is one of the founders of the first professional Ukrainian Theatre, *The Ruska Besida Theater*. In 1862 as an audit student, Kropyvnytskyi attended classes at the Law Faculty of Kiev University. Deeply impressed by a melodrama he saw in Kiev Theatre, he wrote the play "Mykyta Starostenko or You do know when disaster will awake". He later criticized this work as it was an attempt by inexperienced author. Now the play is known in the version, that has undergone numerous fundamental revisions, Kropyvnytskyi had not completed his education for various reasons; one of them he moved to Elisavetgrad, where there was a library. There he got acquainted with Robert Owen, John Stuart Mill, William Shakespeare, Lord Byron, Johann Wolfgang von Goethe, Heinrich Heine, Alexandre Dumas, George Sand and William Makepeace Thackeray among other writers. In his government service he was rarely promoted and often completely lost his earnings due to his devotion for art and amateur performances. In 1871 he joined the troupe of professional actors and agreed to work in the company of Count Morkov, in Odessa. He gained great theatrical experience after spending over ten years in the Russian Theater troupe. In 1872 the Odessa newspaper "Novorossiysk Telegraph" published two musical comedies by him: *Reconciled* and *God will protect an orphan*, or Unexpected Proposal. In 1875, Kropyvnytskyi went on tour in Galicia, where he worked as an actor and director of the theatre company "Ruthenian talk"; there he made some effort to change the repertoire and artistic style of the theatre in bringing it to the realism and national character. In 1881, the ban on Ukrainian theatre was abolished, though there still were many limitations and restrictions, Ukrainian troupes emerged in Kyiv, Kharkiv, and Odessa, yet these troupes did not satisfy Kropyvnytskyi, who sought for dramatic changes in scenic art. In his later years he was restricted due to worsening health to settle in a farm house, but still traveled to participate in theatre performances. Kropyvnytskyi died on 21 April 1910 on his way from Odessa, and was buried in Kharkiv. In July 2016 the city of Kirohvohrad was renamed Kropyvnytskyi in his honor.

Joseph Boskovic

(531)

Joseph Boskovic was born May 18, 1711 in Dubrovnik, Croatia to a Serbian father (Nikola Bošković) and Italian mother (Paola Bettera). His mother was described as a robust and active woman with a happy temperament who lived to 103. Joseph Boskovic was a polymath, scientist, astronomer, mathematician who became a Jesuit priest, theologian, philosopher, diplomat, and member of the Royal Society.

The electrical genius Nikola Tesla made a point that Boskovic had written thousands of volumes on the theory of relativity, including time-space continuum, hundreds of years before Albert Einstein was praised for it. Could Einstein have forgotten to give credit where credit was due? When Einstein was asked how it felt to be the smartest man alive, he replied; "I don't know, you'd have to ask Nikola Tesla."

His education started in Rome, at the Society of Jesus. He became a professor of mathematics at age 29.

In Vienna in 1758 Boskovic published the first edition of his famous work, Philosophiæ naturalis; Theory of Natural Philosophy Derived To The Single Law of Forces Which Exist in Nature. His work is the precursor of the atomic theory. He coined the Law of Force: Repulsive on small inter-electronic distances, and attractive on greater distances (Michael Faraday continued the development of this findings). The

Bohr model of atoms is a direct continuation of Boškovic'es atomic model. His scientific approach solved static issues in construction.

In his works, he offered the image of a super-powerful calculating intelligence, before the French Laplace, who was credited for it.

He was elected to the Royal Society in London in 1761.

Boskovic produced a precursor to the atomic theory and made many contributions to astronomy. A crater on the moon was named after him; The Boskovic(h) Crater. In 1753 he discovered the absence of atmosphere on the Moon. He founded the Brera Observatory (Milan) in 1764.

There are many versions of Boskovic's name; Ruggero Giuseppe Boscovich (Italian), Roger Joseph Boscovich (English), but Ruđer Josip Boškovic was his Serbo- Croatian birth certificate name.

Though his fiery temperament made him enemies, and led him to move around a lot (social awkwardness is often attributed to geniuses), his work was important for masterminds that emerged after him; Einstein, Faraday, Bohr, Laplace, etc.

His legacy is celebrated in Croatia (especially Dubrovnik), Italy and Serbia.

Joseph Boscovic died of age 75 on 13 February 1787.

Svetlana Boskovic
(532)

Svetlana Boškovic was born in Yugoslavia before the civil war tore the country apart. Her father, who had been working in Denmark since the 1980ies in order to create a better future for his family, managed to drive back in the nick of time to pick up his wife and 3 daughters; load up the car, say goodbye to everyone they knew, and cross the Serbian-Hungarian border before the civil war broke out, and the borders closed in June 1991. His loyal older sister (Zora) worked as a translator in Denmark, and paved the way to their new, safe home country.

Svetlana arrived in a foreign country, on one of the smallest islands in Denmark; Fur. With only 820 inhabitants on the island there were more inbred Danes than foreigners.

"Go back to your own country" she was told on a regular basis by the racist kids at school. Bullying and names like "Osama Svetlana" (a reference to the terrorist Osama Bin Laden) along with being called "ugly" led her to spend lunch hours crying in the school restroom; feeling alone and unwanted. Books and animals were her only companions for 6 years, but 3 years after arriving in the country, her Danish teacher raved that she was the best in her class at Danish — as the only foreigner in class!

Even after the war had ended (in 1999) there was nothing to "go back" to. The Clinton Administration had bombed Serbia, the capital state of former Yugoslavia, in order to stop the civil war. Bridges, high rises and radio towers had been bombed. The country was left with damaged infrastructure, which necessitated accepting China's money many years later in order to rebuild. Serbia wasn't able to become a part of EU, so they desperately needed China's money. China's plan was to build a silk road in Europe, starting in Serbia. They purchased massive lithium mines.

Why did NATO bomb Serbia? Because of Milosevic's inhumane killings of muslims in Yugoslavia (especially Bosnia and Croatia caught the eyes of International news media). The Serbian Nationalists wanted to clean up the country after it had been invaded by the Ottoman Empire who pillaged, raped and forced conversion from Orthodox Christianity to Islam 5 centuries ago. Today there are fewer muslims in Serbia than in Denmark.

Svetlana's father was born in March 1945. As a chemistry scientist, he saw no future in Yugoslavia (which was formerly a part of the Austro-Hungarian Empire). He sought work in other countries such as Austria, Iraq, Germany & Denmark. On one of his trips back to Yugoslavia he met Svetlana's mother, a Hungarian Serb. When he tasted her soup, he knew he wanted to marry her.

Svetlana's paternal grandparents, a power couple, had built a trucking empire in Yugoslavia (Serbia), and lived an affluent life before World War 2, but then communism took its grip on Yugoslavia, and stole everything from them. Svetlana's paternal grandfather (Svetozar), whom she was named after because she had his blue eyes, was held at gunpoint and given an ultimatum by the communists; if he didn't surrender his political opposition and his assets, the trigger would be pulled. He had to surrender, or his 8 children would be left without a father. He died before Svetlana was born.

The communists forced themselves into their estate, and stole everything of value that the Boškovic family owned. Because of communism they went from riches to rags.

Svetlana grew up with no sense of belonging; the country she had been born in didn't exist anymore; she knew of the disappointment in her parents that their (combined) 4th and final child wasn't a boy either, and that her sister tilted her baby carrier on purpose so she fell out. She was fed tales by her half sister that her not being born male was when the problems started. She felt like the root of the problem, and unwanted in every way.

During a suicide attempt at age 15, she saw a glimpse of herself traveling freely on the other side of the globe.

"If I'm going to die anyways, I have nothing to lose", she realized, and decided to live out this vision. She packed a few bags, and left her strict and controlling home at age 16, just like her father had.

She taught herself how to overcome shyness and insecurity, and sell with confidence. Instead of partying, she spent her early 20ies on learning online marketing, so she could work anywhere in the world.

In 2012 she arrived in America, and felt at home in this cultural melting pot. For the first time in her life she heard people say that her name was 'beautiful'. In 2014 she felt called to come to Hawaii - just like she had seen in the vision — exactly on the other side of the globe! Hawaii has the exact same core values as Yugoslavia had, and Serbia has:

HOSPITALITY & LOYALTY. The Hawaiian King David Kalākaua created diplomatic relations with the Kingdom of Serbia in 1882. Svetlana's spirit knew there was a sense of belonging here.

Never give up,

dreams do come true,

and God's plans are greater than you think.

Svetlana reads biographies and commentaries of people who made a difference in partnership with Terry Bosgra on the Christian Radio Station K-Light Radio (Hawaii) on radio station 1040AM (not FM) weekdays at 11:05 am HST (Hawaii time) / 3:05 pm MDT / 2:05 pm PDT / 5:05 pm EDT / 23:05 Europe.

She speaks up about how feminism taken too far hurts feminine women and masculine men, and how women can motivate instead of emasculate men, on: ManMotivator.com

Kirsten Neuschafer

(533)

Kirsten Neuschafer was born 23 June 1982 in South Africa and attended Deutsche Internationale Schule (*German International School*) in Pretoria. As a young girl she began sailing dinghies, became a professional sailor, and was attracted to anything that might be a challenge. At age 22 she cycled across Africa from north to south; although her heart was set on navigating the oceans, test her abilities on the water, and began doing charter deliveries taking film crews to places like the Falklands, and the Antarctic Peninsula. Such trips gave her an appetite for greater challenge. In 2023 she was awarded the Rod Stephens Seamanship Trophy by the Cruising Club of America and the Ocean Cruising Club's (OCC) Seamanship Award for a serious rescue operation. She led the fleet since rounding the Cape Horn and became the first woman to win this round the world race. According to the International Association of Cape Horner's Records, Neuschafer has become the seventh woman to circumnavigate the globe solo non stop via the Great Capes in yachts under 18m. Kirsten is the only female skipper and first woman who participated in the 2022 Golden Globe Race (GGR), (*race without stop or any outside assistance*) a retro sailing race in which the entrants single-handedly circumnavigate around the globe, solo, nonstop by using boats designed prior to

1988 and celestial navigation, without the use of modern equipment; cassette tapes are ok but no GPS. She entered that race, (a challenging journey for a young female solo sailor). While in the Indian Ocean she received a distress call from fellow entrant Tapio Lehtinen, (*Finish engineer*) after his boat sank, Kirsten was determined to be the nearest vessel, 100 miles away. Lehtinen had spent over 24 hours adrift in the Southern Indian Ocean; Neuschafer changed course, located, and rescued him then went on to complete the race. Her boat *Minnehaha* is a Cape George 36 built in Port Townsend, Washington, launched in 1988. Kirsten spent a year in Prince Edward Island (PLI) while refitting her boat in preparation for the GGR journey. Some of the islanders who took part in the refitting of *Minnehaha*, included shipwright Eddie Arsenault, who met her on the dock and asked do you need a hand? At the Golden Globe Race, after just over 235 days at sea and a painfully slow final few miles as she ghosted toward the end, crossed the finish line around 10 hours behind competitor Simon Curwen, but a previous stop for repairs for the British sailor had already relegated him to the Chichester class for those who make a single landfall. Kirsten Neuschafer is a fearless lady and made *dreaming the impossible dream* (composed by Mitch Leigh), a reality for her life, rather than singing it, she lived it.

Roy Moore

(534)

Roy Stewart Moore was born 11 Feb. 1947 in Gadsden Alabama, US, the oldest of 5 children having two brothers and two sisters. He attended West Point and served as a company commander in the Military Police Corps during the Vietnam War. He first joined the Democratic Party but in 1992 changed his affiliation to the Republican Party. He married Kayla in 1985 and the two have 4 children. Roy graduated from the United States Military Academy with a BS, and from the University of Alabama with a JD, after that joined the Etowah County district attorney's office. In 1982 was appointed as a Circuit Court Judge. In 2001 he was elected to Chief Justice of the Alabama Supreme Court. After he got that position he installed a 2,000-kilogram (*4,400 lb*) monument in the rotunda at the state judicial building inscribed with the *Ten Commandments*. That was too much to accept by the "*anti Religious police*". The issue of Christianity in public had already been debated several times, most notably during the *1962 prayer in school* case when the US Supreme Court officially outlawed prayer in US public schools. More controversy erupted when a Federal judge ruled the Ten Commandments are in violation of the US Constitution. Judge Moore argued that the display had nothing to do with religion, but a Federal judge overruled that and ordered judge Moore to remove the monument, which he refused to comply and lost his case against attorneys of the _Southern Poverty Law Center_ (SPLC) and was suspended from office. Christian groups (including me), met with Judge Moore in Washington DC and rallied behind him. Moore campaigned for his position and was re-elected in 2013 by the people of Alabama, with 913,021 votes as chief justice again, but resigned in 2017 to run for the US Senate replacing the vacated seat of Jeff Sessions. At that point he was accused by three women claiming that he had sexually assaulted them at their respective ages of 14, 16, and 28. President Donald Trump endorsed Moore. He attracted national media attention about his views opposing homosexuality, transgender, as well as being a leading voice in the birther movement where he said that Barrack Obama was not born in the United States. One powerful argument was that according to Sheriff Arapio the Obama birth certificate of Kapiolani Hospital was changed several times, (_our children & grandchildren are all born in that hospital_). After his military service he lived one year in Australia fulfilling a longtime desire to see the outback, there he worked at the Telemon ranch near Springsure. Those who knew him there spoke highly of Moore, although one commented "I don't think he'd ever done that sort of manual labor in his life." In August 2022, Moore was awarded $8.2 million in a defamation lawsuit against a Democratic aligned super PAC.

Kenny Poure

(535)

Kenny Poure was born in Long Beach California where his father was in the automobile business and asked him to take a group of junior high boys to camp and offered Kenny to take that new Cadillac on the lot; it's a few hours driving but Kenny was an entertaining guy and these young boys were all going to camp. It was in the year of 1959 when Arthur Fleming was the secretary of Health, Education, and Welfare, and he advised the world that cranberries were contaminated thereby scaring the population about the dangers of consuming cranberries; even Mamie Eisenhower advised the White House had discontinued serving cranberries on toast replacing it with applesauce for thanksgiving dinner. What Fleming failed to point out was that one would have to eat 15,000 pounds of cranberries every day for several years to get cancer. *The Great Cranberry* scare created havoc at the worst possible time in 1958; it is a popular item at the thanksgiving dinners. Shortly thereafter we arrived in Calif. and remember the aftermath of that was still reverberating. We arrived in Long Beach and were warned about the serious health risk of cranberries and did heed that warning for several years after that; although it was new to us as we had family members in New Zealand involved in cranberry and blueberry production. Kenny Poure accepted his fathers offer and took a carload of junior high boys to Hume Lake Camp in California. For him it was the beginning of a new direction that changed his life from car sales to a youth counselor. He was asked to be on staff at the camp and shortly thereafter the board asked Kenny & Melba to be the executive directors. It was there that we met them and began a long time friendship that lasted many years. We invited him to Hawaii as a speaker for a youth conference, and according to our guestbook he stayed as our house guest during the week of 29 March 1979. He spoke at several meetings; Kenny was gifted with a strong ability to reach 12 and 14 year old young people. I told him God blest you with a rare gift of skillfully communicating to youth of that age. He was a funny and the youth loved him; Kenny said, I relate to them, they really are _pre-people_. After meetings other speakers would rest at our home over a cup of coffee, but not Kenny, he was in the pool with the youth acting like one of them, just a big kid. We were richly best by his visit. When our children reached the Junior-high age we took them to Hume Lake Camp. Dr John Mac Arthur was the speaker; Kenny and Melba invited Mr. Mrs. Mac Arthur and Pamela & me to a private dinner in their home. He was an entertaining speaker and led many people to Christ in his life. Kenny Poure died on 18 Oct. 2014. We have fond memories of him he impacted the lives of many and modeled a life of fun and joy walking with Jesus. It's sad there was only one of him.

Kellyanne Conway

(536)

Kellyanne Fitzpatrick was born on 20 Jan. 1967, in New Jersey US. Her father's ancestry was German, English & Irish, and her mother is of Italian descent. Her parents divorced when she was three and Kellyanne was raised by her mother, grandmother, and two unmarried aunts. She went to St Joseph High School and graduated as a class valedictorian, sang in the choir, played field hockey, worked on floats for parades, and was a cheerleader. She worked eight summers on a blueberry farm and at age 20 she won the world Champion Blueberry Packing competition, everything she learned about business started on the farm. She graduated magna cum laude with a BA in political science from Trinity College in Washington DC, (*now Trinity Washington University*); there she was elected to Phi Beta Kappa. She earned a Juris Doctor with honors from the George Washington University Law School in 1992. After graduation she served as a judicial clerk for Judge Richard A. Levie of the Superior Court at the District of Columbia. After graduating she worked for Frank Luntz, (Political and Communication Consultant and Pollster) begun there while a student at Trinity College. She lived and served on the condo-board of the Trump Tower, there got to know Donald Trump. At first she endorsed Ted Cruz and criticized Trump's use of eminent domain, saying he bulldozed over the little guy to get his way. In

2016 Cruz suspended his campaign and Trump hired Conway as a senior advisor, after Paul Manafort resigned, Trump named Conway the third campaign manager. She served in that capacity for 10 weeks through the November eight general election and was the first woman to successfully run an American Presidential Campaign. In December Conway appeared on a forum where tempers began to flare escalating into a shouting match; Hillary Clinton's senior strategist said; more Americans voted for her than for Trump, to which Conway replied "Hey guys we won, you don't have to respond, he was the better candidate, that's why he won." Shortly after that she was receiving death threats, and for that Trump assigned the secret service to protect her. She got America one of the greatest presidents of all time elected, but her husband George was a strong critique of Trump and campaigned against him. George and Kellyanne are both attorneys and work on opposite sides of the political spectrum therefore let's not speculate what the dinner conversation topics may have been in their home. Although (considering their work schedule there may not have been too many. The Conway's have 4 children together therefore there must have been some agreement from time to time. In March 2023, George and Kellyanne Conway announced that they were divorcing after 22 years of marriage, a high price to pay for two successful careers.

Nellie Bly

(537)

Elizabeth Jane Cochran was born 5 May, 1864 in Pennsylvania, US, and became known by her pen name Nelly Bly; she was 13th daughter of 15 children, at age 6 her father died. In 1885 she was 21 when a column was published titled: "What girls are good for" stated that girls are principally good for birthing and keeping house. It prompted her to write a response under the pseudonym "Lonely orphan girl". The editor George Madden was impressed with her passion he ran a advertisement asking the author to identify herself and offered her an opportunity to write a piece for the newspaper. She accepted and her first article in the Dispatch was titled "The Girl puzzle" argued not all women would marry, what was needed were better jobs for women. Her 2nd article was titled Mad Marriages published under the byline "Nelly Bly" character in a popular song. It was customary for women writers to use pen names. Her editor wrote Nelly Bly by mistake, after the popular song by Stephen Foster, but the error stuck. Madden was impressed with her writing and offered her a full time job. As a writer she focused her early work on the lives of working women, writing a series of investigative articles on women factory workers. The newspaper soon received complaints from factory owners and she was reassigned to the women's pages to cover fashion, society, and gardening. She soon became bored and decided to do something no girl had done before. She traveled to Mexico to serve as a foreign correspondent, spending half a year reporting on lives and customs of Mexican people. Her dispatches were published in a book. She protested the imprisonment of a local journalist for criticizing the Mexican government. When the authorities learned about it they planned to arrest her, but she fled the country. In New York City she faced rejection after rejection due to the fact that most editors would not consider hiring a woman. Penniless after 4 months, she talked her way into the offices of Joseph Pulitzer's newspaper, and took an undercover assignment for which she agreed to feign insanity to investigate reports of brutality at the Women's Lunatic Asylum. She stayed up all night to give her the wide-eyed look of a disturbed woman. After being checked in she refused to go to bed, and landed in court. She was examined by a doctor and re-committed and experienced the deplorable conditions first hand. Her reports were published in book form it ushered her into an era of stunt girl journalism. After that she went *Eighty days around the world* making the fiction into a reality. She wrote stories about Europe and on World War-I and was the first woman to visit the war zone between Serbia & Austria. On 27 Jan. 1922 she died of pneumonia at age 57 in New York and was honored with her picture on a postage stamp, she was inducted into the National Women's hall of Fame.

Richard Bong

(538)

Richard "Dick" Ira Bong was born 24 Sept. 1920 in Wisconsin US, first of 9 children born to Carl Bong (*Swedish immigrant*) and Dora Bryce. Dick grew up on a farm in Wisconsin where he became interested in aircraft watching planes fly over the farm carrying mail for President Calvin Coolidge's summer White House. Bong entered Poplar High where he played the clarinet, played baseball, basketball and hockey, graduating in 1938, then took pilot training. In 1941 he enlisted in the Army Air Corps Aviation Cadet Program. One of his flight instructors was Captain Barry Goldwater who later became the US Senator from Arizona. His ability as a fighter pilot was recognized while training in Northern California. He was commissioned second lieutenant and awarded his wings in 1942. Then he flew very low "buzzed" the house of a friend who had just been married. He and a few friends had flown very low at Market street in San Francisco and blew a woman's clothes of the line, was cited and temporarily grounded for breaking flying rules and reprimanded for that by General George Kenney, who later wrote "We needed kids like this lad". Bong denied flying under the Golden Gate Bridge although was grounded for it while his group was sent to England, he was sent in opposite direction and flown as a passenger aboard a B-24 Liberator from Hawaii via Hickam

Field to Australia. Upon arrival he was assigned to the P-38 fighter unit, and was transferred several more times; while on leave he met Marjorie and adorned the nose of his aircraft with her photo. In the Pacific theater he shot down his 26th and 27th Japanese aircraft surpassing Rickenbacker's record of 26 in WW-1. Bong was promoted to Major by General Kenney and dispatched to the US where was given leave and did a 15 state bond promotion tour and returned to New Guinea and was assigned to the V Fighter Command staff as an instructor with permission to go on missions but not seek combat. He continued flying from Tacloban, Leyte during the Philippines campaign and by December he increased his air-air victory claims to 40. His gunnery accuracy was poor, but compensated for that by getting close to the target, in some cases flew through the debris of exploding enemy aircrafts and on one occasion collided with his target. On recommendation of General Kenney he received the Medal of Honor from General Douglas MacArthur. After that he became test pilot assigned to Lockheed. Then on 6 August 1945 he had already flown four hours in the P-80 when the fuel pump malfunctioned during takeoff; Bong ejected but was too low for his parachute to deploy the plane crashed and Richard Bong died at age 24; his death was front page news across the country sharing space with the bombing of Hiroshima.

Antony Armstrong-Jones

(539)

Antony Charles Robert Armstrong-Jones, 1st Earl of Snowden was born 7 March 1930 in London England. He was an only son and was called Tony. His parents divorced before his first birthday. Tony contracted Polio as a teenager and the illness took a toll on one of his legs, resulting in the fact that he was limping for the remainder of his life; he was educated at 2 private boarding schools, and went to Eton College where he qualified in the extra special weight class of the school boxing finals. He then matriculated at the University of Cambridge, where he studied architecture at Jesus College but failed his 2nd year exam, and began a career as a photographer in fashion design and theatre. His portraits were highly favored among them were official portraits of Queen Elizabeth II and the Duke of Edinburgh during their tour of Canada. In February 1960 he became engaged to the Queen's sister Princess Margaret, and they married on 6 May 1960 at Westminster Abby. It was the first ceremony to be broadcast on television. Despite the enthusiasm of the public, critics did not approve of a commoner marrying in to the royal family, nevertheless the couple made their home in Kensington Palace. He became Earl of Snowden, and they had 2 children Earl David and Lady Sarah. Sadly the marriage began to collapse quite early due to a variety of causes;

Margaret was into late night partying while Snowden had an undisguised sexual addiction, (summed up by a friend), "*if it moves he'll have it.*" Both had their problems, like most of us, and the couple remained married for 18 years. They were both strong-willed and accustomed to having their own way. His work consumed a great deal of time, and she expected more of that time. When it became obvious that this was not an enduring matrimony, they separated. When life is an open book, (as certainly is in the case with British Royalty), people have opinions on how those who live inside the Palace should conduct themselves, your life is a public event, and Tony knew that before he stepped into it. Most people, including the Royal Family, took his side. Tony & Margaret separated in 1976 and the marriage ended in divorce in 1978. During his royal marriage, he was patron of the National Youth Theatre, The Contemporary Art Society for Wales, the Welsh Theatre Company. He was President of the British Theatre Museum. He was a council member of the Polio Research Fund and served as a trustee of the National Fund for Research into Crippling Diseases. Tony Armstrong Jones died 13 January 2017 at age 86 in Kensington London England, and was survived by his 2nd wife Lucy.

Beth Holloway

(540)

Elizabeth Ann Reynolds was born in 1960 in Arkansas. She married David Holloway. They had a daughter named Natalee, and a boy Matthew born in Tennessee. Divorced in 1993, Beth raised both children. She later married George *"Jug"* Twitty, a businessman and moved to Alabama. In Dec. 2009 Jug filed for divorce. Beth and the children stayed in Birmingham. In May 2005 Natalee graduated from high school and the class traveled to Aruba. They returned May 30, but Natalee failed to check in for her flight and was last seen outside a nightclub in Oranjestad with local boys Joran Vander Sloot and brothers Deepak and Satish Kalpoe. Immediately after Jug & Beth flew to Aruba by private jet and presented the Aruba police with the name Joran Vander Sloot as the person with whom Natalee left the nightclub. The manager at the Holliday Inn recognized Joran on the tape. Then with two policemen they went to the home of Vander Sloot, who initially denied knowing Natalee, changed their story and said they dropped Natalee at her hotel around 2 AM. Beth alleged in a TV interview that these boys knew more than they told and that at least one of them raped her daughter. Beth got copies of police reports that Joran admitted having sex with Natalie at his home. Vinda de Sousa, (Holloway's Aruba atty.) understood it might have been consensual sex, although police commissioner Gerald Dompig denied any such statements were made. Joran and the Kalpoe brothers were arrested. Beth got more frustrated and said I am no further than the day I got here, and referred to the boys as criminals. That evening a demonstration of 200 Arubans took place in Oranjestad, with signs: <u>*Innocent till proven guilty*</u>, <u>*respect our laws*</u>, or <u>*go home*</u>, the lawyer for the boy's threatened legal action. Later Beth discovered that Joran Vander Sloot and his father Paul were on a flight to New York; as they stepped off the plane were handed a lawsuit, but threw it away indicating no regard for the law. Dutch television picked up the story showing Joran smoking Marijuana admitting he was there when Natalee died. It became the most watched program. (During the 1950's I lived 3 years <u>*in a very different Aruba*</u>) Beth believes Paul Vander Sloot orchestrated a cover up. Joran contacted Beth and said for $250,000 he would reveal all and said his father had buried the body in the foundation of a house. The FBI got involved & set up an Aruba sting, but determined that the house did not exist; the Birmingham court charged Joran with fraud and distortion. Beth discovered that Joran was in a Peru prison for murdering 21 year old <u>*Stephany Flores*</u> Bet flew to Peru, visited the prison and spoke to Joran who would only see her with his lawyer. In May 2023 Peruvian officials reported that Joran is serving a 28 year prison term for murder and will extradite him to Alabama; this story is far from over.

Boris Johnson
(541)

Boris Johnson was born 19 June 1964 in New York to Stanley & Charlotte Johnson who studied at Columbia University. Later that year they returned to England so Charlotte could study at Oxford. In 1966 they relocated to Washington DC; in 1969 the family returned to England and settled in Somerset. Stanley enjoyed fox hunting and was often absent leaving the children to be raised by his wife. As a child Boris was quiet, studious, and deaf, resulting in several ear operations; his earliest ambition was to be "<u>World King</u>". In 1970 the 4 children attended Primrose Hill Primary School. Stanley secured a position in Brussels, there the children learned French, but Charlotte had a nervous breakdown, was treated for clinical depression and the children were sent to Ashdown House, a preparatory boarding school in East Sussex, England. There he played rugby, studied ancient Greek and Latin, but was appalled about corporal punishment. In 1980 his parents divorced and the children moved in with mom. Boris got a King's Scholarship to Eton College a boarding school near Windsor, after that he used his middle name <u>Boris</u>, and developed an eccentric English persona, for which he became famous. He changed from <u>Catholic</u> to <u>Church of England</u>. School reports that he was <u>idle</u>, <u>often late</u> but were <u>popular</u> and <u>well known</u> at Eton.

His friends were from the wealthy upper class. He excelled in English and the classics, was in the school debate society and editor of the newspaper *The Eton College Chronicle*. He went for a year to Australia where he taught English and Latin in an elite boarding school, in Geelong; he won a scholarship to study Literae Humaniories at Balliol College Oxford; a four year course in the study of the classics, ancient languages, literature & history, and ancient and modern philosophy. He was one of the Oxford undergraduates who later dominated British politics and media such as Nick Boles, David Cameron, Michael Gove, and others to become senior Conservative Party politicians. In Sept.1987 Johnson married Mostyn-Owen, they honeymooned in Egypt, and upon return settled in Kensington west London; he began working at the leadership writing desk of *The Daily Telegraph*. His articles appealed to middle England readership. In 1989 he was assigned to Brussels and wrote about the European Union change, Fall of the he Berlin Wall, the French and Germans had to decide how to respond. What was Europe going to become? In 2001 he won a seat in Parliament, in 2003 he visited Baghdad; in 2004 he backed unsuccessful proceedings to impeach Tony Blair. In 2007 He was elected to Mayor of London, in that position he was embroiled in the contentious issue of Brexit, resulting in the historic vote of June 23, 2016 to leave the EU, served as Prime Minister, authored several books, one of them; *The Churchill Factor*.

Ava Kolker

(542)

Ava Grace Kolker was born 5 December, 2006 in Los Angeles California, the family moved to Florida, but later returned to California. Ava has three sisters, Kayla, Jade & Lexy Kolker. Early in her life she became a child star in the Disney movie series, and so did her sister Lexy. Ava began acting at a very young age and starred in *Girl meets world* (2014-2017), *Sydney to the Max* (2019-2021), *Scary movie 5* (2013), *Miss Meadows* (2014), *Message from the King* (2016), *The Last Key* (2018) She began her acting career in 2011 at age 5. Disney had the unique ability to attract very young children and was able to develop them as talented actors & actresses; many people love to see talented young children, on the movie screen. (*see #461 in Book 3 in this series*); Ava made her debut with a guest appearance on the television. A year later, she appeared in her first film, starring as Marybeth Geitzen in the comedy film *Golden Winter*. Following that she was cast as Lily in the comedy film series *Scary Movie*. She was in the final installment in the series. Commercially the series was a great success. The same year she appeared in drama film *The trial of Cate McCall* as Agie. She played Heather in the film *Meadows.* Kolker made various guest appearances on television series such as *Dads*, *Sam & Cat* and *Blakish*. In 2015 she was cast in the recurring role of

Ava Morgenstern on Disney Channel's comedy television series *Girl Meets World* the spin-off to *Boy Meets World*. For the role she received the Young Artist Award nomination. In the following year she appeared in murder mystery stories. In 2017 she made guest appearances on the comedy series *White Famous* as Maddie and the superhero series Agents of *S.H.I.E.L.D.* as 12-year old Robin, portraying an older version of the character that was played by her sister Lexy as an 8 year old. In 2018 Kolker was cast on the Disney Channel sitcom *Sydney to the Max* playing the main character of Olive, In the same year she appeared as young Elise Rainier in the film *Insidious*: (*it is the story of a married couple who recently moved in to a new home with their sons Dalton and Foster and their infant daughter Cali. One evening Dalton sneaks into the attic where he encounters a mysterious entity. The next day he inexplicably slips in to a coma. Was hospitalized but did not come out of it and the family took him home, but a series of strange events followed, noises in the walls, security alarm going of on its own, Dalton walking around in comatose condition, etc.*) In 2019 she was cast in a minor role in the film *Red Shoes and the Seven Dwarfs*, released in 2020. she also appeared in *The Good Ones*, in 2019. She appeared in *Eventually*, and *When will it be Tomorrow.* Ava Kolker is still young and has already been starring in more then 11 movies, and is gifted and talented.

Hayley Mills

(543)

Hayley Catherine Rose Vivien Mills was born 18 April 1946 in London England. She was discovered at age 12 and began her acting career as a child and was hailed as a promising newcomer winning the BAFTA award for most promising newcomer for her performance in the British Drama film *Tiger Bay* (1959), the Academy Juvenile award for Disney's *Pollyanna* (1960) and Golden Globe Award for New Star of the Year–Actress in 1961. During her early career she appeared in six films for Walt Disney including her dual role as twins Susan and Sharon in the film *The Parent Trap* (1961). Her performance in *Whistle Down the Wind* (a 1961 an adaptation of the novel written by her mother, saw Mills nominated for the BAFTA Award for best British actress, and was voted the biggest star in Britain for 1961. She was a top movie star for about a decade. In the late 1960's Mills began performing in theatrical plays, making her stage debut in a 1969 West End revival of *Peter Pan*, she began to play in more mature roles and received the Disney Legend Award. Although she did not maintain the Hollywood box office A-List as a child actress. She has continued to make films and TV appearances including maintain a starring role in the UK; in 2021 she published her memoirs *Forever Young*. During her first six year run with Disney she was arguably the most popular child actress of that era. Critics noted that Americas favorite child star was in fact quite British and very ladylike. Mills wrote in her memoir; it gave me the career but hampered me from getting more different kind of roles. At age 21 she lost her Disney fortune to a 90% tax rate implemented by the Inland Revenue in England. Her appeal to regain her funds was shot down, and Mills admitted that she was worried about going the path of Judy Garland (*successful American actress, who began as a child star but was affected by constant criticism, so much so, she began abusing drugs & alcohol which ultimately led to overdose and her death in 1969.*) Once the pinnacle of success is reached as a teenager, do they have the maturity to move forward into adulthood? A hungry world out there often wants more with no concern for the well being of the star that may not have more to give. In 1966 at age 20 while filming *The Family Way* she met and married 53 year old Roy Boulting; they owned a flat in London and had two boys but the marriage only lasted 6 years after that Hayley only had partners. In April 2008 Mills was diagnosed with breast cancer, had surgery but abandoned chemotherapy after only three sessions because of the severity of side-effects. She told Good Housekeeping Magazine in 2012 that she had fully recovered. In the past she has delved into Hinduism and Christianity for guidance, she is now in her high seventies and we do not know what she practices today.

Carissa Moore

(544)

Carissa Moore was born 27 August, 1992 in Honolulu Hawaii. When she was five years old she began surfing with her dad off the beaches of Waikiki. Her father Chris was a competitive open water swimmer who won a number of competitions. He lived closer to the water than her landlocked mother. Her parents divorced when she was ten years old. When Carissa stayed with her mother, the motivation for surfing would start to wane, and wrote letters to her father to stay motivated. She started earning multiple wins at National Scholastic Surfing Association, NSSA, junior surf competition at age 11 she clinched a record 11 NSSA amateur titles and at age 16 in 2008 she became the youngest champion at a Triple Crown of Surfing event when she won the Reef Hawaiian Pro. In 2010, Moore qualified to compete on the ASP (now called World Surf League) Championship Tour. She won two major contests, finished third overall, and was named Rookie of the Year. The following season, Carissa was a youngster to watch on the World Tour and she lived up to her reputation, winning three events and claiming her World Crown unseating four time defending champion Stephanie Gilmore in the process. At age 18 she became the youngest person – male or female – to win a surfing world title. She took top World Tour honors again in

2013 and 2015. Moore was named an Adventurer of the year by National Geographic, a Woman of the Year by Glamour magazine and Top Female Surfer in the SURFER magazine poll (numerous times). She was inducted into the Surfers' Hall of Fame and the State of Hawaii declared January 4 to be Carissa Moore Day. At the 2019 World Surf League Women's Championship Tour, Moore finished in first place and qualified for the 2020 Summer Olympics. In the Tokyo Summer Olympics Moore competed under the Flag of the United States for the first time in her career, it was also her first time to participate in the Olympic games. In the first round she won her heat which advanced her to the third round. The 2020 Summer Olympics were the first Olympic Games where surfing was included as a sport and Carissa Moore became the first woman in history to win an Olympic gold medal in surfing. She won the WSL finals in 2021. Moore is of Irish German descent through her father, while her mother is Native Hawaiian and Filipino. Moore is a 2010 graduate of Punahou School and married her high school sweetheart, Luke Untermann in December 2017. Shark attack survivor Bethany Hamilton wrote that she admired Moore's toughness when they competed as nine year olds.

Stephanie Gilmore

(545)

Stephanie Louise Gilmore was born 29 January 1988 in New South Wales Australia and goes by the name Steph. At age 9 she began surfing and at 17 she was entering world tour events as a wild card competitor which paid of with a victory at the 2005 Roxy Pro Gold Coast. In her next season she won another wild card event the 2006 Hawaianas Beachley Classic, Gilmore's success on the World Qualifying Series (WQS) tour qualified her for the 2007 Women's ASP World Tour and she did not disappoint. She won four of the eight events and claimed the 2007 World Title. She would repeat her success in 2008, 2009, 2010, 2012, 2014 and 2018. Gilmore also won the inaugural Swatch Girls Pro France in 2010, and that same year 2010 she was inducted into the Surfers Hall of Fame and won the Laureus World Action Sportsperson of the year award. In 2014 she was the top athlete on the ROXY Surf Team. In that same year Stephanie starred in a feature-length documentary titled "*Stephanie in the Water*". She qualified for the Tokyo 2020 Olympics. She had a bye in Round 2 but was then beaten by Bianca Buitendag from South Africa in Round 3 and did not contest for the medal. Australia at the 2020 Summer Olympics details the results in depth. Although the 2007 season was Gilmore's rookie year, she captured the Foster ASP Women's World Title. She won three events in 2007 to enter the final event of the season, the Billabong Pro Maui, ranked in first place; when the other contenders former world champion Sofia Mulanovich and sophomore Silvana Lima bowed out before her, she won the title. Our children & grandchildren as well as many friend are surfers and living here on a hill 1 block from the ocean they are always standing in our living room and attempt to get some glimpses of the waves; if its good, of they go. The place to be is not our living room but take a drive to the North Shore. We ourselves are not surfers, but love to watch the professionals. Watching a film she had made in Hawaii, we are more & more aware of the fact that no matter what happens, surfing will have a warm place in our hearts. Raw honest surfing is alive especially here in Hawaii and in Australia and South-Africa will never go extinct. There's something intangibly special about watching Stephanie connect with the wave and subsequently demolish it; she is so smooth and rides these waves in the most aesthetically pleasing way. She's always happy and seems to glide through the waves the way she talks. Stephanie has adopted the gift that was past on to us by our Polynesian ancestors and seems to have forgotten how complex it is. The list of her World Tour wins is way to long to print here; it's a pleasure to watch her comments on the airwaves after the wins. The way she talks is the way she rides the waves.

Charlie Wedemeyer
(546)

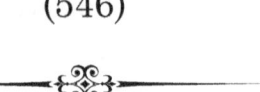

Charlie Wedemeyer was born on 19 Feb. 1945 in Honolulu the youngest of nine children to Bill and Ruth Wedemeyer. Charlie was a high school athlete and quarterback of the Punahou School football team, and named Hawaii Prep Athlete of the decade in the 1960's; in 1964 he was named ILH player of the year and played a playoff game against Kamehameha that was televised. After graduation in 1965 he attended Michigan State Univ. where he played for Coach Duffy Daugherty. Charlie graduated from Michigan State in 1969 and obtained a masters degree from Central Michigan University. After graduating and getting married they settled in Los Gatos, California had 2 children Carri and Kale. Charlie was a math teacher at Los Gatos High in, and was the head football coach there. In 1976 while writing math problems on the chalkboard in class he started dropping the chalk, followed by similar problems with his hands and sought medical advice. He was diagnosed with Amyotrophic Lateral Sclerosis, (ALS) aka <u>Lou Gehrig's disease</u>. It begins with weakness in the arms and legs followed by difficulty speaking or swallowing. 90% such cases have no cause, there is no known cure for it. He married Lucy Dangler, his high school sweetheart, and Charlie was given one year to live. Charlie & Lucy prayed that he could see their children grow up to graduate from high school and college. <u>They did</u>; Carri runs the website for the Family outreach program which raises money for ALS research, and Kale is a medical doctor in private practice, both are happily married and live 5 minutes away from their parents. Charlie's greatest accomplishment came as football coach at Los Gatos High School winning seven league championships and posing 78-18-1 record after he was afflicted with ALS in 1985, his team won the Central Coast Section Championship with Lucy on the sidelines, reading his lips and relaying his plays to assistant coaches. Charlie said when adversity is insurmountable, God has given us freedom of choice: We can choose to feel sorry for ourselves, be bitter and angry, and cause everybody to be miserable, or we can become a stronger and better person for it; pain and suffering are inevitable – we all experience it; but misery is an option; we get to make that choice. Charlie was always upbeat, when he spoke at the Oahu Community Correctional Center he quipped "*<u>I too have a life sentence.</u>*" We met Charley, he had a contagious smile on his face and left us smiling. He underwent two major surgeries, but his kidneys failed him and Charlie died in Calif. at age 64 on 3 June 2010. Lucy said: *<u>God is good, we have been blessed,</u>* her dear friend Suzanne Maurer wrote; Charlie's home-going has been a painful adjustment for Lucy, many focus on her heavy burden of care-giving, but Lucy said: "*<u>He was the love of my life</u>*".

Isabella Abbott

(547)

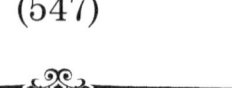

Isabella Aiona Abbott was born on 20 June 1919 in Hana Maui, Territory of Hawaii. Her Hawaiian name means "white rain of Hana" and she was known as "*Izzy*"; her father was ethnically Chinese while her mother was a Native Hawaiian. Her mother taught her about edible Hawaiian Seaweeds, and the value and diversity of Hawaii's native plants. Abbott was the only girl and second youngest in a family of eight siblings. She grew up in Waikiki, and graduated from Kamehameha Schools in 1937, and received her undergraduate degree in botany at the University of Hawaii in Manoa in 1941, a master's degree in botany from the University of Michigan in 1942, and a PhD in botany from the University of California, Berkeley in 1950. She married zoologist Donald Putnam Abbott who had been a fellow student at the University of Hawaii as well as Berkeley. The couple moved to Pacific Grove, California where he taught at the Hopkins Marine Station run by Stanford University. At that time women were rarely considered for academic posts she spent time raising her daughter Annie Abbott Foerster while studying the algae of the California coast. In 1966 she became a research associate and taught as a lecturer at Hopkins. She compiled a book on marine algae of the Monterey peninsula, which later was expanded to include the entire California coast, and was awarded the Darbaker Prize by the Botanical Society of America in 1969. By 1972 Stanford University promoted her directly to full professor of Biology where she was the first woman and first person of color in this position. In 1982 both Abbotts retired and moved back to Hawaii where she was hired by the University of Hawaii to teach ethnobotany, the interaction of humans and plants. She authored eight books and over 150 publications. She is considered the worlds leading expert on Hawaiian Seaweeds, known in the Hawaiian language as *Limu*. She has been credited with discovering over 200 species, with several named after her, including Rhodomelaceae family (red algae) genus of *Abbottella.* It earned her the nickname "First Lady of Limu". In 1993 she received the Charles Reed Bishop Medal and in 1997 she received the Gilbert Morgan Smith Medal from the National Academy of Sciences. She was the G.P. Wilder Professor of Botany from 1980 till she retired in 1982. She was the foremost authority on the algae of the Pacific Ocean basin, and was awarded the lifetime achievement award from the Hawaii Department of Land and Natural Resources for her studies of coral reefs. Isabella Kauakea Aiona Abbott died at age 91 on 28 October 2010 in her home in Honolulu. To preserve her legacy a research ethnobotany and marine botany scholarship was established in her honor.

Chad Kalepa Baybayan
(548)

Chad Kalepa Baybayan was born 15 Aug. 1956 in Honolulu, to Llewellyn Baybayan Sr. and Lillian Suter. The family moved to Lahaina Maui where he grew up living there till he was 39. He held a master's degree in education and was fluent in the Hawaiian language, and dedicated his life to community, education, Hawaiian Culture, exploration and voyaging. He was a teacher, leader, and believed that a *Hokule'a* was a vehicle to carry the values of kindness, compassion and generosity. When asked about sailing on Hokule'a, he said it's about stewardship, aloha, building good and healthy relationships, and life-long friendships, it's about committing to the idea of aloha and service to your community. He saw *Hokule'a* as a symbol for successful aspirations and a promise for all that is possible. It is a reminder of all that we have accomplished in the face of enormous adversity. He first sailed on Hokule'a in 1975 and participated on all major Hokule'a voyages since 1980, including 18 legs of the Malama Honua Worldwide Voyage; he served as captain on the voyages of *Hawai'iloa* and *Hokualaka'i*. His first voyage to Tahiti in 1976 was marked by troubles and he learned a lot, some of the crew faced unexpected difficulties managing four and as half weeks of life onboard an isolated vessel which continued to amplify after making landfall. These conflicts ultimately led navigator Mau

Piailug, to exit the adventure and not take part in the return trip to Hawaii. The intent of these voyages were a revival of traditional voyaging of the ancient Polynesian cultures without any modern navigational equipment, Kalepa lived his whole life in his ancestral roots reaching deep into the islands past history, culture, and practice, his forefathers who came here navigated by the stars. In 2007 on the Micronesian Island of Satawai his teacher master navigator Mau Piailug initiated him in the two thousand year old Micronesian Society of deep sea navigators. Kalepa had learned all the mistakes of the early Tahiti voyage. The goals were to revive and re-awaken a culture that after years of their people had been suppressed and needed revival. What they faced was that the crew members who had trained for the voyage, men and women, were of many different backgrounds, they were – Chinese, Filipino, Hawaiian, Portuguese, English and American. Not quite the indigenous Hawaiian-Polynesian people. Kalepa's success in developing unity from diversity involved leadership, training, and supporting each and every participant. He became well known and respected both in Hawaii and around the world as a master navigator of the 62-foot double-hulled Hokule'a. Chad Kalepa and his wife were in Seattle to be with their 6 year old grandson who was undergoing chemotherapy. There she found Chad unresponsive on the floor, unable to revive him, he died at age 64, on 8 April 2021 in Seattle.

Nainoa Thompson

(549)

Charles Nainoa Thompson was born 11 March 1953 in Honolulu Hawaii. He is a descendant of Kamehameha-1, graduated from Punahou School in 1972 and earned a BA in Ocean Science in 1986 from the Univ. of Hawaii, where he was trained by master navigator Mau Piailug from the island of Satawal in the solitary coral atoll in the Yap state of Micronesia. Thompson is best known as the first Hawaiian to bring back the ancient navigation art of the Polynesians not used since the 14th century; having navigated two double-hulled canoes, the Hokule'a and the Hawai'iloa from Hawaii to other Island nations in Polynesia without the aid of western instruments. His first voyage was from Hawaii to Tahiti in 1980. Since then he has been a lead navigator on subsequent voyages of Hokule'a including the voyage of Rediscovery from 1985-1987. In 2007 Thompson was inducted into Pwo as master navigator. In June 2014 he was made a commander of the Order of Tahiti Nui for his work with the Polynesian Voyaging Society. Thompson serves as Chair of the Board of Trustees for Kamehameha Schools (a post that his father Myron "_Pinky_" Thompson also held), and a member of the Board of Regents for the Univ. of Hawaii. His autobiography is framed by "_The Ocean is my Classroom_" written by Gisela E. Speidel, Editor of the Kamehameha Journal of

Education, and Kristina Inn, Associate Editor, taken from two speeches by Nainoa Thompson. Thompson has inspired and led a revival of the traditional voyaging arts of Polynesia navigating; he had a passion to practice the art of *Wayfinding* on long distance ocean voyaging, in 1980 he became the first Hawaiian, and the first Polynesian, to revive an art that had ended around the fourteenth century. Thompson grew up on his grandfather's dairy & chicken farm in Niu Valley when it was still country. Yoshio Kawano, the milkman introduced Nainoa to the ocean. He would sit on Yoshio doorstep at dawn, waiting to take him fishing. To 5 yr old Nainoa, that was very special. Nainoa learned from Yoshio, from Dad, from Mom, from Grandma and Grandpa, he learned from those who loved him and showed him kindness. Family did not push competition, that came in school; I used to ask why *this* book? Why *that* book? Why are we learning about dead people in far away countries? It was important, but hard for me to trust teachers until I got to the fifth grade of Mrs. Hefty, she fully understood Nainoa and they *still* correspond with each other today. After he graduated from Punahou he went fishing for a while; but then he started to paddle outrigger canoes at the Canoe Club, it was like the lights came on, the ocean was huge, wild, free, and open. The Hokule'a is sixty-two feet long and nineteen feet wide, carries a load of 26,000 pounds; after she was launched, Nainoa Thompson was its first navigator.

Mau Piailug

(550)

Pius "Mau" Piailug was born in 1932 in the Carolinian Island Weiso, Satawal Yap, South Sea Island, Federated States of Micronesia. Mau is best known as a teacher of traditional non-instrument wayfinding methods for open-ocean voyaging. His Carolinian navigation system relies on using the Sun, Stars, Winds, Clouds, Seas, Swells, Birds and Fish, acquired through learning passed down with teaching in the oral tradition. He earned the title of master navigator (*palu*) at age eighteen. As he neared middle age, Mau grew concerned that the practice of navigation in Satawal would disappear as his people became accuculturated to Western values. Hoping that the navigational tradition would be preserved for future generations, Mau shared his knowledge with the Polynesian Voyaging Society (PVS), and with his help they used experimental archeology to recreate and test lost Hawaiian navigational techniques on the *Hokule'a* which is a modern re-construction of a double-hulled Hawaiian voyaging canoe. The successful non-instrument sailing of *Hokule'a* to Tahiti proved the efficacy of Mau's navigational system to the world. To academia Mau's achievement provided evidence for intentional two-way voyaging throughout Oceania, supporting a hypothesis that explained the Asiatic origin of Polynesians. The Micronesian-Polynesian cultural exchanged symbolized by *Hokule'a* had an impact throughout the Pacific, with a revival of Polynesian canoe building in Hawaii, New Zealand, Rarotonga and Tahiti. Later in life, Mau was respectfully known as a grandmaster navigator and was called "*Papa Mau*" with reverence and affection; he received an honorary degree from the University of Hawaii, and was honored by the Smithsonian Institution and the Bishop Museum for his contribution to maritime history. The legacy of Mau lives on in several books and documentary films and is remembered by the indigenous people of Oceania. After becoming a navigator Mau married Nemwaeito with whom he raised ten boys and six girls. They caught fish, raised chicken and pork, for their source of protein. A freshwater pond served as bathing facilities Mau's daily village life involved harvesting taro, coconut, and breadfruit. (*In the 1960's we invited Micronesian students from the University to our home. In the yard had a large breadfruit tree always loaded with fruit; they climbed that tree and harvested the fruits. We did not like the taste but to them it was a delicacy.* According to these students local materials were used to construct outrigger canoes called *proa*. American missionaries arrived after World War II and built the first church and school. Mau's contributions to wayfinding sparked cultural pride in Tahitians, Maori and Hawaiians by connecting Polynesians to their forbearers. Mau Piailug died at age 78 in Satawal Yap, on 12 July 2010 in Micronesia.

C. J. Walker

(551)

Madam C. J. Walker was born Sarah Breedlove on 23 Dec. 1867 in Louisiana US. She had 5 siblings an older sister and 4 brothers. Sarah was the 1st child in her family born into freedom after President Abraham Lincoln signed the Emancipation Proclamation. Her mother died in 1872; her father died a year later, and Sara was orphaned at the age of seven. At 10 she moved in with her sister Louvenia and brother-in-law Jesse Powel. She had only 3 months of formal education. In 1882 at 14, (*to escape from Jessie Powell*), she married Moses Mc Williams. They had one daughter A'Lelia, who was born 6 June 1885. Sarah was 20 when Moses died and A'Lelia was two. In Jan. 1906 Sarah married Charles Joseph Walker, a newspaper advertising salesman and she became Madam C. J. Walker, but divorced in 1912; Lelia adopted her stepfather's surname and became known as A'Lelia Walker. Walker was Christian and philanthropy oriented. In 1888 Sarah moved to St. Louis where three of her brothers lived. Sarah worked as a laundress for a dollar a day. In 1888 she sang at St Paul African Methodist Episcopal Church and started to yearn for an educated life as she watched the women at her church. She suffered severe dandruff and other scalp ailments including baldness due to skin disorder, poor diet, infrequent bathing, with no indoor plumbing, heating and electricity. Her brothers were barbers and Sarah became a commission agent selling hair-care products for Annie Malone, an African American hair care entrepreneur millionaire and owner of the Poro Company. Sarah began to take her new knowledge, developed her own product line, and moved to Denver. Malone accused Sarah of stealing her formula, which had really been around for centuries. Sarah became known as Madam Walker; in 1906 her daughter took charge of mail order operations in Denver, while she and her husband relocated to Pennsylvania and opened a beauty parlor. When A' Lelia moved there and took it over, Sarah moved to Indianapolis, set up a factory there which became the headquarters producing mainly hair growth products. Her business increased with much of the prophets going to philanthropy. By 1917 she had trained about 20,000 women. Her first national conference that year was attended by 200 women entrepreneurs. She addressed the first annual gathering of the <u>National Negro Business League</u> and said: "*I am a woman who came from the cotton fields of the South, was promoted to the washtub and then to the kitchen, from there, I promoted myself into the business of manufacturing hair goods and built a factory on my own ground.*" The following year in 1918 she was the keynote speaker, and on 25 May, 1919 she died from kidney failure at age 51, and bequeathed $100,000 to orphanages and two-thirds of all future prophets to charity.

Ed Parker

(552)

Edmund Kealoha Parker was born 19 March, 1931 in Honolulu Hawaii. He was enrolled in Judo classes by his father at age 12, and received his Shodan in 1949 at age 18. After receiving his brown belt in Kenpo he moved to Brigham Young University in Utah where he began to teach martial arts; his Kenpo Shodan diploma is dated 1953. Parker's book *Kenpo Karate*, (as it was called), published in 1961 show many hard linear movements. All the influences up to that time were reflected in his rigid linear method of "*Kenpo Karate*" later when he was influenced by the Chinese arts he included that information in his system. Kenpo Karate is one of the oldest forms of martial arts that originated in India, while there are many styles of martial arts; Kenpo Karate is the only art that integrates all four ways of fighting. After leaving the Coast Guard and finishing his education at BYU, Ed settled in Southern California. There he was surrounded by other martial artists from a wide variety of systems, many willing to discuss and share with him. Some of them were Ark Wong, Haumea Lefiti, Jimmy Wing Woo (who developed many of the American Kenpo forms still in use today), Jimmy H. Woo, (Chin Siu Dek), founder and Grandmaster of Kung Fu San Soo (Tsoi Li Ho Fut) and Lau Bun. These martial artists were known for their skills in arts such as *Five Family*

Fist Kung Fu, *Splashing-Hands*, *San Soo*, *Tai Chi*, and *Hung Gar*, and his influence remains visible in both historical material, (*such as forms that Parker taught in his system*) and current principles. He was significantly influenced by the Japanese and Okinawan interpretations prevalent in Hawaii. Parker was well known for his business creativity and helped many martial artists open their own dojos. He was known in Hollywood where he trained some stunt men. He served as one of Elvis Presley's body guards during the singer's final years. He is best known as the founder of American Kenpo and is referred to fondly as the "*Father of American Kenpo*." He is formally referred to as Senior Grandmaster of American Kenpo. He opened the first karate school in the Western United States in Provo Utah in 1954. By 1956 he opened a dojo in Pasadena California, his very first black-belt was James Ibrao, his first brown belt student was Charles Beeder; (there is some controversy over the fact that Beeder received the first black belt awarded after Ed Parker had moved to California). In 1962 John McSweeney opened a school in Ireland which prompted Parker to give control of the Kenpo Karate Association of America to the Tracy Brothers create a new organization *The International Kempo Karate Organization*. Ed Parker died of a heart attack at age 59 on 15 December 1990, after arriving at Honolulu International Airport.

Emmeline Pankhurst

(553)

Emmeline Pankhurst Goulden was born 15 July 1858 in Manchester England, and she grew up in the Moss Side district to politically active parents. There was some controversy about the exact date of her birth, but she claims 15 July (as stated here), is the correct date of her birth. (*The controversy was feeling a kinship with the female revolutionaries who on 14 July 1789 stormed the Bastille in Paris, although at that time the prison only had seven inmates, all were set free, the revolution was about the monarchy's abuse of power, which was the flashpoint of the French Revolution.*) Her teachers called her Emily which she preferred. The family into which she was born had been steeped in political agitations for generations; Emily was introduced at the age of 14 into the women suffrage movement. In 1878 at her age 20 she began a relationship with Richard Pankhurst age 44 and her mother chastised her for throwing herself at Richard, resulting in a later wedding in 1879. Emily attended to Richard but much of her time was taken up with the suffrage movement; in their first 10 years she gave birth to 5 children, she and Richard both believed that she should not be a *"household machine"*, and hired a butler to help with the children. In 1886 they moved to London where Richard made an unsuccessful attempt for Parliament. She opened a small fabric shop together with her sister Mary. In 1888 their son Frank developed diphtheria and died. Soon after that they had another son and named him Francis in honor of his diseased brother; then moved to a more affluent district making their home a center for political activists, socialists, protesters, suffragists and free-thinkers. They hosted many VIP guests including foreign visitors. Political parties split and in 1888 Britain's first nationwide coalition of groups advocating women's right to vote was formed, but it was a splintered group. Some believed that married women did not need this since their husband voted for them. Then Emily and her husband organized another group to advocate for married women but wanted this party for all women married and unmarried, named the _Women's Franchise League_ (WFL). There they ran in to roadblocks again as it supported equal rights for women in the areas of <u>divorce</u> and <u>inheritance</u> resulting in many disagreements. There were hurdles and hoops to overcome such as <u>property rights</u>, but the lights came on and _<u>Women's right to vote</u>_ was finally on its way to become a reality with few hurdles to be conquered, such as <u>equal marriage laws</u>, <u>equal pay for equal work</u>, <u>equal job opportunities for all</u>. Years of traveling, lecturing, imprisonment and hunger strikes had taken their toll, with fatigue and illness; her health deteriorated and on Thursday 14 June 1928 she died at age 69 in London. Women can vote but some paid a high price for such rights.

Ka'iulani

(554)

Ka'iulani was born on 16 Oct.1875 in Honolulu and was the only child of Princess Miriam Likelike & Scottish businessman Archibald Scott Cleghorn and was the last heir apparent to the throne of the Hawaiian Kingdom; her uncle was king Kalakaua. At the christening ceremony she was named Victoria Kawekiu Ka'iulani, Kalaninuiahilapalapa Cleghorn. In her teens she was an expert equestrian, with her friend Eva Parker, and was an avid surfer, (*may have been the first surfer*), she said my mother taught me to swim before I could walk. As a child she was acquainted with *Robert Luis Stevenson* who used to take her on long walks when he visited. After the death of her mother, Princess Ka'iulani was sent to Europe at age 13, leaving in 1889 for England, along with half sister Annie, and Mary Matilda Walker, (*wife of the British vice-consul*) under the guardianship of businessman Theo H. Davies to England. There she became highly educated in the arts, got fluent in the languages, all to prepare her for royal duties before age 18. But the 1893 overthrow of the Hawaiian Kingdom drastically altered her life. The committee of safety rejected proposals to seat princess Ka'iulani on the throne. She went to President Cleveland and 1st lady Frances, but her efforts were in vain. The situation put both Ka'iulani and her father in dire financial straits. Her annual government stipend ceased, and her father's income as a govt. employee came to an end. She left Hawaii as a <u>princess</u> and returned as a <u>pauper</u>. Father and daughter spent 1893-1897 drifting among European aristocracy, relatives and friends in England, Wales, Scotland and Paris, but it became clear; *<u>they were royals without a kingdom</u>*, and returned to Hawaii, settling in to life as private citizens. She and Lili'uokalani busied themselves with social engagements and mourned the loss of Hawaiian Independence. On December 14, 1898 she visited ranch owner Samuel Parker for the wedding of his daughter Eva, who was her childhood friend, both loved horseback riding, and were galloping in pleasant weather, which soon turned into a windy rainstorm with no raincoat, the weather at the ranch in high elevation is substantially cooler. After returning to the ranch *<u>Ka'iulani</u>* fell ill, upon learning about it, her father sailed there on the steamship *<u>Kinau</u>* with the family physician, but her condition deteriorated and she could only be moved on a stretcher. On Monday 6 March, 1899 Ka'iulani died at age 23 of inflammatory rheumatism at her Ainahou home, from there her body was moved to Kawaiahao Church where she lay in state, after which her remains were interred with that of her mother at the Royal Mausoleum in Nuuanu. In the late eighteen hundreds the senses showed 29000 total residents; the Advertiser estimated 20,000 lined the streets for her final journey.

Abigail Kawananakoa

(555)

Abigail Kinoiki Kekaulike Kawananakoa was born 23 April 1926 in Honolulu, Territory of Hawaii. She was an only child of Lydia Liliuokalani Kawananakoa and William Jeremiah Ellerbrock. The Kingdom of Hawaii's last two monarchs, Kalakaua and Lili'uokalani were childless; because of this, both monarchs named family members as heirs. Abigail was educated at Punahou school in Honolulu, the Shanghai American School in Shanghai, (1938-1939), and Notre Dame High School in Belmont, California, from which she graduated in 1943. She attended Dominican College in San Rafael California (1943-1944) and studied at University of Hawaii in 1945. At age six she was adopted by her grandmother, Princess Abigail Campbell Kawananakoa with the intention she remain a direct heir to a possible restoration of the kingdom. She is a granddaughter of Prince David Kawananakoa the adopted son of King Kalakaua. With the adoption by her grandmother Abigail became a daughter of Prince Kawananakoa, thereby establishing her as a member of the Hawaiian Royal family. Jon M. Van Dyke, a University of Hawaii law professor states in his book: _Who owns the Crown Lands of Hawaii?_ That the Kawananakoas view themselves as the designated heirs of the Kalakaua Line, though none of them have ever claimed an interest in the Crown Lands.

Kawananakoa was an expert horsewoman and owner of ranches in Hawaii, California, and Washington State. She was a 20-year cumulative breeder of AQHA quarter horses winning many victories. Kawananakoa was the president of the "*Friends of Iolani Palace*" from 1971 to 1998, succeeding her mother who founded the organization. The palace was built by her adopted great-granduncle King David Kalakaua. She was active in various causes for the preservation of native Hawaiian culture, including the restoration of Iolani Palace. She was heiress to the largest estate of her great-grandfather, James Campbell a 19th century industrialist from Ireland. When in 2007 the estate was converted her share was estimated to be about $250 million. She supported the Thirty Meter Telescope protest aimed at preventing its construction. She has been supportive of the Polynesian Voyaging Society. In 2017 she had a medical episode, in a handwritten note to the media she explained firing her former attorney James Wright, First Hawaiian Bank succeeded him. Kawananakoa died of complications of a stroke at age 96 on 11 December, 2022 at her home in Nu'uanu, The governor of Hawaii ordered all flags to be flown at half staff out of respect for her; she was buried at the Royal Mausoleum in Nu'uanu. Abigail Kawananakoa was not official royalty but was often referred to with the title of Princess.

Rell Sunn

(556)

Rell Kapolioka'ehukai Sunn was born on 31 July, 1950 in Makaha Hawaii, her middle name means *the heart of the sea*, was given to Rell by her grandmother. Her legal birth name was Roella, a combination of her parent's names *Roen* and *Elbert Sunn*. She disliked it and eventually changed it to Rell. Her father was a beach boy, a term for men who were some mix of a lifeguard, surfing instructor, and tourist guide. She began surfing at the age of 4, and was Hawaii's number one female amateur surfer for five years and was Hawaii's first female lifeguard. In 1966 she accompanied Duke Kahanamoku on a trip to California to attend a world championship, from then she began traveling around the world to compete professionally. In the late 1960's she moved to Oklahoma where she got married and had one daughter, Jan Sunn-Carreira. In 1972 the marriage failed, and she and her daughter returned to Hawaii. After a five year hiatus from surfing, she returned to surf. By 1995 remarried to her third husband, Dave Parmenter, a professional surfer and board shaper. With few other women, Sun co-founded the Women's International Surfing Association, (WISA) in 1975; In 1979, she along with Jericho Poppler, Lynne Boyer, Margo Oberg, Cherie Gross, Linda Davoli, Debbie Bacham, Becky Benson and Brenda Scott, formed Women Pro Surfing

(WPS). In 1982 Sunn ranked number one in the world on longboard. In 1982 during a pro surf meet in Huntington Beach Calif. Sunn felt a lump in her breast while drying off during the competition; it turned out to be <u>advanced stage breast cancer</u>. At age 32 she was diagnosed and given a prognosis of one year. Sunn continued to surf daily despite the pain from bouts of chemotherapy, radiation treatments, medications and the financial toll associated with the disease. Following her diagnosis, Sunn became a radio disc jockey and surf reporter, a physical therapist at Waianae care home, and a counselor at a cancer research center. She helped pilot a program for breast cancer awareness at the Wai'anae Cancer Research Center that involved educating local women about the causes and prevention of breast cancer. Over the next 14 years, her cancer went into remission three times, and she underwent a mastectomy and bone marrow transplant, but the disease eventually spread to her brain. In the 1980's she began her own surf competition; <u>Rell Sunn Menehune Surf Contest</u>, which is held annually in her hometown of Makaha in the hopes of encouraging sportsmanship and environmental awareness in a community that experiences a high juvenile delinquency rate. Rell Sunn eventually lost her battle with cancer and died at age 47, on 2 January, 1998; her ashes were scattered in the ocean at Makaha, attended by 3,000 people.

Paul Revere

(557)

Paul Revere was born 1 January 1735 in Boston British America; (*some records that show his birth date at 21 December, 1734; due to the fact that there were 2 different calendars in use that time, we were not there, and let you decide on the correct date*). His father Apollos Rivoire a French Huguenot had come to Boston. In 1729 Rivoire anglicized his name to Paul Revere and married Deborah Hitchborn a member of a long standing Boston family that owned a small shipping wharf. Their son Paul Revere was the 3rd of twelve children, but never learned his father's native language, at age 13 he was apprenticed to John Coney the silversmith a trade that afforded him connections with a cross section of Boston society. He became active in the American Revolution, but rather than the Puritan services he was drawn to the Church of England and became one of the new bell ringers. His father died in 1754 when Paul was too young to take over the family shop. In February 1756 during the French Indian war he enlisted in the provincial army, after that he returned and assumed control of the silver shop in his own name. On 4 August 1757 he married Sarah Orne, after she died he married Rachel Walker, both wives gave him 8 children each. In the next 7 years Revere's business suffered severely due to the war. It got so bad he lost his shop in 1785, and to help make ends meet Revere took up dentistry, a skill he was taught by a practicing surgeon who lodged at a friend's house. One client Joseph Warren and Revere became close friends they had the same political views. From 1773 to Nov.1775, Revere served as a courier for the Boston Committee of Public Safety traveling between New York and Philadelphia, and reported on the political unrest in Boston. Research shows 18 such rides. When Boston was besieged after the battles of Lexington and Concord, Revere could not return to the city which was firmly in British hands. He tried but was denied a commission in the Continental Army then found other ways to be useful and became a courier. His friend Joseph Warren was killed in the battle of Bunker Hill on 17 June, 1775. What Paul Revere is best known for is the all night ride of 18 April 1775 warning patriots along his route, many of whom set out on horseback to deliver warnings of their own. By the end of the night there were probably as many as 40 riders carrying the news to the army. Revere did not shout the phrase as has been attributed to him: "*The British are coming*" his mission depended on secrecy; the countryside was filled with British army patrols. According to his own account, he narrowly escaped capture, and some reports show he was captured. The system was so effective that people within 25 miles were aware of British troop movements within hours. Paul Revere Died 10 May 1818 in Boston, at 83; Rachel died 5 years earlier.

Pearl Kupe

(558)

Dr Pearl Kupe is born and raised in South Africa and I count her as one of my very best friends, especially on the continent of Africa I can likely count those who I know that well there on the fingers of one hand. Pearl is an amazing girl and is known over most of the world. She is an attorney, a global speaker, an author, a business entrepreneur and an international consultant. I am connected with, and serve on, an International Humanitarian organization called Global Hope Network International, which is headquartered in Geneva Switzerland with offices in Jordan, Scotland, Orlando, Colorado, California and Hawaii, for about 5 years or so I served as chairman of the board of directors. It was on that committee where I was blest to meet Dr Pearl Kupe who represented South Africa there. We met about once a year for a few days and really got to know our members who came from four corners of the globe, and my interest was generally who we could attract from the continent of Africa. Pearl was certainly one of the brightest stars on the block and when we were meeting over a weekend or holiday and not be in reserved mode where things could get rather tense sometimes, but on off time we could respond to each other in more of a relaxed fashion and (so too speak) "_let our hair down_" it was then that someone like Pearl Kupe would light up the party. One day we agreed on a relaxing day, rented a bus, and visited the picturesque French Alpine resort town of Chamonix it's about 3,500 ft elevation located near Mount Blanc in the French Alps, and on the one hour bus ride, in a more relaxed frame of mind, we needed someone like Pearl who was gifted to serve as a special entertainer for such a trip. Professionally Pearl earned her LLB, Bachelor of Laws from the University of Botswana (in conjunction with Edinburgh University) and her doctorate conferred by ACTS Institutes India. She has served as Senior State & Principal State Counsel in the Botswana Attorney General Counsel and was the first appointed registrar to the Botswana Industrial Labor Court has worked as Social Dialogue Specialist; Pearl Kupe speaks at many global conferences on a number of different topics that pertain to the African continent, relating to transformational leadership, Social dialogue and labor law issues, specially those that concern women; she is also a consultant to ministry of Labor, Kingdom of Swaziland, and is a leader in the pro-life movement. Having worked with Pearl internationally I would like to be one of the first to join her fan club. God made only one Pearl Kupe and I feel privileged to have for sometime been counted as one connected to her inner circle. Her list of accomplishments and involvements would fill the pages of this book.

James Dobson

(559)

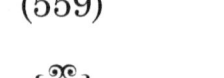

James Clayton Dobson Jr. was born 21 April, 1936 in Shreveport Louisiana US. He told a reporter that religion played a central part of his life, he learned to pray before he learned to talk, and gave his life to Jesus at the age of three, in response to an altar call by his father who was a Nazarene minister which had been a family tradition for several generations. Instead of following *that* he became an evangelical Christian Author, psychologist and founder of Focus on the Family which he led from 1977-2010, broadcasting in more than a dozen languages on over 7,000 stations worldwide, reportedly heard by more than 220 million people in 164 countries. In the 1980s he was ranked as the most influential spokesman for conservative social positions in American public life. In August 1990 at age 54 Dobson suffered a mild heart attack; after a brief hospital stay he was back. He may not have been an ordained minister, but was called "_the nation's most influential evangelical leader_" by New York Times. He studied academic psychology at Pasadena College (_now Point Loma University in San Diego_), and got his doctorate from the University of Southern California and became an Associate Clinical Professor of Pediatrics at the University of Southern California School of Medicine for 14 years; and spent 17 years on the staff of the Children's

Hospital Los Angeles in the Division of Child Development & Medical Genetics; he worked at the Institute of Family Relations, (*a marriage-counseling center in Los Angeles*). He interviewed serial killer Ted Bundy who claimed to have been influenced by violent pornography, while he raped and murdered 30 young women; Dobson called for Bundy to be forgiven. The Bundy tapes generated over $1-million revenue for Focus on the family, (of which $600,000 was donated to anti pornography and pro-life groups). In 2003 Dobson stepped down as CEO of Focus on the Family and resigned from the position of Chairman of the Board in Feb. 2009. He said *the biggest mistake a founder and president can make is to stay too long, by holding the reigns of power.* Dobson married Shirley on 26 Aug. 1960, they have two children Danae and Ryan. After removing himself from Focus on the Family, he founded radio program "*Family Talk.*" In 2008 he was inducted in the Radio Hall of Fame. He supports private school vouchers with tax credit, is very strong pro-life. Initially he remained somewhat distant from Washington Politics, but then founded *Family Research Counsel* in 1983, articulating and advancing a family centered philosophy in public life providing research and analyses primarily in Washington. Dobson has written 36 books on family related issues. We had the privilege of meeting Dr Dobson on more then one occasion.

Margarita Louis-Dreyfus

(560)

Margarita Olegovna Bogdanova was born 1 July 1962 in Leningrad Russian SFSR, Soviet Union. She was raised by her grandfather, (an electrical engineer), and studied law in Moscow, and economics in Leningrad. In 1988 on a Zurich to London flight she met Robert Louis Dreyfus, dated him for a few years, and married him in 1992; they had 3 boys including Kyril who is chairman and majority shareholder of English Championship football club, Sunderland. Margarita, who had been working for a circuit-board equipment seller, became a full-time wife and mother. Her husband Robert Louis-Dreyfus was stricken with leukemia, and died on 4 July, 2009, and she took over as chairman of the Louis Dreyfus group, actually became heir to the group; as well as majority shareholder of Olympique de Marseille, a football club her husband had owned since 1996. Her husband Robert had integrated her into the management of the group in 2007, when he learned of his illness. On 29 August 2016, Luis-Dreyfus and the Marseille mayor, Jean-Claude Gaudin, stated during a press conference with Frank McCourt that McCourt had agreed in principle to purchase the *French Ligue-1 football club, Olympique de Marseille*, owned by Louis-Dreyfus. The purchase deal was completed for a reported price tag of 45 million euros on 17 October

2016. She kept 5% of the club as part of the deal. Football has become the most visible sport in the world. We see it through the World Cup, the (English) Premier League which has created a fantastic business model. In the year 2016 her net worth was estimated at $9.5 billion. She is a Swiss citizen living in Zurich with her 3 sons, Eric born in 1992, and twins Maurice and Kyril born in 1997; she lives with her partner Philipp Hildebrand, former head of the Swiss Central Bank; she gave birth to twin girls on 21 March 2016. Margarita is the 2nd cousin once removed (by marriage) of American actress Julia Louis Dreyfus. According to the French Press the Russian-born businesswoman, dubbed the "Tsarina" has not always been so wealthy, after Robert Luis –Dreyfus died from Leukemia a few years later her life took another turn as she took over the reins at his commodities company and met a new partner—the former head of the Swiss National Bank, and in March 2016 she gave birth to twin girls. Why do millionaires and billionaires live in Switzerland and not in Russia or America? (According to Hank Vreedenburg, Vice President of Chase Manhattan Bank who owned a condo in Hawaii and was a very personal friend), that issue goes back to the days of Charlie Chaplain who pioneered a special tax deal with the Swiss Government, which is now rather common for successful and wealthy people that otherwise would get fleeced by their respective countries.

Clara Schumann

(561)

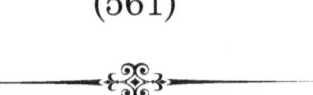

Clara Josephine Wieck was born to Friedrich and Mariane Wieck on 13 Sept. 1819 in Leipzig, kingdom of Saxony, German Confederation. Both parents were pianists and piano teachers and her mother was a singer. Clara was trained by her father, who planned her career to the smallest details; she started receiving basic piano instruction from her mother beginning at four. After her mother moved out, she began daily one hour lessons from her father, which included subjects such as piano, violin, singing, composition, theory, counterpoints, and harmony. She had to practice for two hours every day. Her musical studies came largely at the expense of a general education, although she studied religion and languages under her father's control. Clara made her official debut on 28 Oct. 1828 at the Gewandhaus in Leipzig, she was nine, and the same year she performed at the Leipzig home of Ernst Carus, director of the mental hospital at Colditz Castle. There she met Robert Schumann, another gifted young pianist who had been invited to the musical evening; he admired her music so much he asked permission from his mother to stop studying law, which had never interested him, and take music lessons with Clara's father. He rented a room in the Wieck household and stayed a year; Clara began touring at age eleven and was successful in Paris, Vienna, and other cities. Robert Schumann was nine years older, when at her age 18 he proposed to her and she accepted. He then went to her father for approval but Friedrich opposed it and refused permission. Robert and Clara went to court and the judge allowed the marriage which took place on 12 September 1840, (the day before Clara's 21st birthday), at Leipzig in the Gedachniskirche at her age 20. Clara and composer Robert Schumann had eight children, (*as far as we know her father never changed his mind*). They met and encouraged Johannes Brahms and maintained a close relationship with him. She gave the public premieres of many works by her husband and by Brahms. In February 1854, Robert Schumann had a mental collapse, and attempted suicide he was admitted to a sanatorium near Bonn where he stayed till he died two years later. She continued touring with violinist Joseph Joachim and other chamber musicians. Beginning in 1878, she became an influential piano educator at Dr, Hoch's Konservatorium in Frankfurt; there she attracted international students. In addition Clara continued with her concert tours; Brahms composed some piano pieces to console her. She played her last public concert 12 March 1891 and on 26 March 1896, Clara Schumann suffered a stroke and died less than 2 months later on 20 May at age 76, but her music lives on. The grand piano along with her own picture, are featured on the 100 DM banknote in Germany.

Alphabetical Page Book 4

Abigail Kawananakoa: (555)
Adam Smith: (487)
Al Harrington: (507)
Alina: (505)
Allan Bakke: (518)
Ann Coulter: (522)
Antony Armstrong-Jones: (539)
Arthur Lindsley: (517)
Asha de Vos: (449)
Athanasius: (451)
Ava Kolker: (542)
Beth Holloway: (540)
Boris Johnson: (541)
Briet Bjarnhedinsdottir: (482)
Brother Andrew: (467)
C. J. Walker: (551)
Carissa Moore: (544)
Chad Kalepa Baybayan: (548)
Charles Hodge: (489)
Charles Stanley: (513)
Charlie Wedemeyer: (546)
Chloe Cole: (527)
Christopher Rufo: (455)
Clara Schumann: (561)
Claude Pepper: (461)
Constantine the Great: (471)

D, James Kennedy: (493)
Danny Kaleikini: (504)
Don Knotts: (497)
Ed Parker: (552)
Eddie Aikau: (514)
Emma Lazarus: (496)
Emma Veary: (501)
Emmeline Pankhurst: (553)
Ernest Cassutto: (521)
Eva Peron: (515)
Everett Dirksen: (469)
Frank Pavone: (528)
Frederic Chopin: (479)
Gabby Pahinui: (525)
Gerard Van Groningen: (529)
Giorgia Meloni: (464)
Giuseppe Verdi: (477)
Gladys West: (470)
Hans Egede: (481)
Hayley Mills: (543)
Irving Berlin: (490)
Isabella Abbott: (547)
Israel Kamakawiwo'ole: (500)
J. Gresham Machen: (512)
James Dobson: (559)
James Guthrie: (495)

James O'Keefe: (498)
James Renwick: (492)
Jerome: (491)
Johann Sebastian Bach: (474)
John Wesley: (472)
John Winthrop: (485)
Joseph Boskovic: (531)
Joseph Haydn: (476)
Ka'iulani: (554)
Kate Middleton: (459)
Kayleigh Mc Enany: (452)
Kellyanne Conway: (536)
Kenny Poure: (535)
Kirsten Flagstad: (502)
Kirsten Neuschafer: (533)
Klaas Runia: (524)
Kristan Hawkins: (503)
Kyle Rittenhouse: (453)
Ludwig II of Bavaria: (520)
Marcus Aurelius: (473)
Margarita Louis-Dreyfus: (560
Margrethe II, Queen of Denmark: (465)
Maria Bartiromo: (523)
Marko Kropyvnytskyi: (530)
Mary, Crown Princess of Denmark: (466)
Mau Piailug: (550)
Melania Trump: (484)
Michelle Wie: (526)
Monica Gill: (454)
Nainoa Thompson: (549)
Nana Voitenko: (506)

Nellie Bly: (537)
Ngozi Fulani: (478)
Norman Geisler: (458)
Oliver North: (499)
Orrin Hatch: (456)
Pat Boone: (488)
Paul Revere: (557)
Pearl Kupe: (558)
Queen Elizabeth II: (463)
R. C. Sproul: (516)
Richard Bong: (538)
Ron Menor: (511)
Roy Moore: (534)
Shannon Bream: (460)
Sirimavo Bandaranaike: (509)
Soren Kierkegaard: (462)
Stephanie Gilmore: (545)
Svetlana Boskovic: (532)
Theodore Beza: (480)
Tjerk Hiddes de Vries: (450)
Tulsi Gabbard: (468)
Vance Havner: (510)
Vigdis Finnbogadottir: (483)
Vishal Mangalwadi: (519)
Walter Williams: (494)
William Prescott: (486)
William Wrigley Jr.: (457)
Wolfgang Amadeus Mozart: (475)
Yeonmi Park: (508)

www.ingramcontent.com/pod-product-compliance
Lightning Source LLC
Chambersburg PA
CBHW031711060426
42557CB00008B/238